**Writing
Characters
Who'll Keep Readers
Captivated**

NAIL YOUR NOVEL

Roz Morris

ISBN-13: 978-1489567420

ISBN-10: 1489567429

Published by Red Season

Okay, that's the warning stuff over. Now enjoy writing.

Electronic editions of this book are available from Amazon, Smashwords, the ibookstore, B&N and Kobo

NailYourNovel.com

NAIL YOUR NOVEL

Writing
characters
who'll keep readers
captivated

Roz Morris

Also by Roz Morris

*Nail Your Novel: Why Writers Abandon Books & How You Can
Draft, Fix & Finish With Confidence*

*Writing Plots With Drama, Depth & Heart:
Nail Your Novel 3*

Fiction

*My Memories of a Future Life
Lifeform Three*

Contents

9 Character design: questionnaires and other development games 161

Introduction

The main reason readers keep turning the pages of a novel is to find out what happens next. But what happens to whom? It's the characters who make us care.

Compelling novels are about people we're drawn to read about. People who deserve to be at the centre of a story. People who keep us captivated even when they do questionable things.

In 20 years of writing and coaching, I've assessed a lot of novels in progress. I've seen characters who demanded attention from first glance, and stayed alive long after the final page. Equally

I've seen writers go badly wrong, but with excellent intentions. Their plot makes the characters into unthinking puppets. Their iconic everyman is a bland nobody. Their troubled protagonist is an annoying whiner. Their mysterious stranger is a nonentity. Their tender lovers are soppy and cloying. All the characters seem roughly the same except for their names. And sex scenes... well let's not scare everyone just yet.

I've seen novels where I can't tell who's who. The fictional people are well drawn but they are all clones, with perhaps a variation in hair colour, job description or gender.

These problems can all be fixed – and sometimes the fix is a question of nuance rather than wholescale nuke.

This book is structured as a series of tutorials that tackle these fundamental problems. It is an in-depth examination of what goes wrong, why and what to do instead. Section by section, it will build your awareness of how characters drive fiction, how readers respond to them and what works for your kind of novel – whether that's breathless thrillers or literary character studies. What's more, your plot will flow more naturally because you'll create people who make you want to tell stories. The sections will help you troubleshoot a manuscript in progress, and exercises at the end will guide you to populate a new book from scratch.

Of course, you might want to disregard conventions and what is 'accepted'. An awkward effect I'm discussing may be exactly what you want the reader to feel. Nothing here is a prohibition. Art thrives on rule-breakers and mavericks. This book will teach you what works and how. Dip in and read one piece a day. Or dig in for an intensive journey of discovery.

Who am I?

You'll have seen my novels in the bestseller charts, but you won't have seen my name because I was a ghostwriter, hired to write books as other people. I'm now coming out of the shadows with my own fiction.

As well as writing, I have an extensive background in publishing and editing. I've appraised manuscripts for a London literary consultancy and also as a freelance, and my clients include winners of prestigious national awards. From my work with authors I wrote the other books in this series, *Nail Your Novel: Why Writers Abandon Books and How You Can Draft, Fix and Finish With Confidence,* and *Writing Plots With Drama, Depth and Heart.* Others are in the works.

1 Most commonly repeated advice: show not tell

The advice I write most frequently in manuscript appraisals, even to seasoned authors, is: 'don't tell us; show us'. Showing, rather than telling, is a basic tool for bringing a story to life, especially the characters. Whole books are devoted to its many forms and uses, and I'll be mentioning it a lot. So for now, here's a simple explanation.

This is telling:

Otto is fun.

This is a statement made by the author. Contrast with (from Christopher Isherwood's *Goodbye to Berlin*):

Otto has a face like a very ripe peach. He has small sparkling eyes, full of naughtiness.

This is a description that lets, you, the reader, decide that Otto is fun. It is persuasive and memorable. (By the way, there's nothing wrong with writing 'Otto is fun' and then following it with his peachlike countenance and twinkly peepers. For some narratives that will run more smoothly than the description on its own. But in isolation, the sentence 'Otto is fun' does not bring him to life.)

Here's another example of telling:

David was multitalented.

Compare it with:

David had a master's degree in chemical engineering, so he seemed an unusual choice as editor of a prestigious literary journal. Nevertheless he had doubled its circulation in six months. He was a crack shot with a pistol and every year challenged himself to learn to sing the principal tenor role of an entire opera.

When I read this, I'm convinced that David is multitalented.

Telling isn't forbidden, of course. It has distinct uses, depending on the emphasis you want. But when a writer tells, they have made the judgement for the reader. When a writer shows, they offer the evidence and let the reader decide that the character is fun, talented, beautiful, mean, cruel, generous or troubled. The reader owns the judgement and remembers it because they made it themselves.

Which is exactly how we form conclusions about flesh-and-blood people.

Here are two tips to help you show, not tell.

Remind yourself to switch to showing

Showing instead of telling is a habit you have to develop. And even seasoned writers need to be reminded.

Why? Because showing takes mental sweat. It requires the writer to live the scene alongside the characters. Telling is much less demanding – and incredibly easy to do by default.

It doesn't help that much of the preparation work we do is summaries. If we sketch out characters beforehand, we usually write a string of facts or intentions – 'Bill doesn't like snakes', 'Steve is in love with Lucy', 'Tiffany resents the White Witch'. Small wonder that when we write the text, we continue in telling mode. It helps to make sure our notes include 'shown' examples instead of 'told' ones, but we need to make a conscious switch to this more vivid state of immersion.

Your outline and notes can tell; but when you write the text, it's time to show.

Writers also tell instead of show because they worry we won't see characters the way they intend.

Here's an example from a scene where an author wanted us to feel the strain of characters at loggerheads on a family holiday:

Maggie could feel the tension between her brother and his wife. She felt sorry for her brother because his wife seemed so difficult and stuck in her ways.

These lines would be fine if supported by other observations. Otherwise, they're not enough. They are the judgement – but the reader wants the evidence.

How did this tension look? Was there a prickly silence at the breakfast table? Were the couple bickering about the best way to pack the deckchairs into the car and taking no notice when Maggie offered suggestions?

A scene like this is pressing the reader to agree with the writer's view of the characters. The writer gives only conclusions – 'difficult', 'tense', 'stuck in her ways'. This can make the reader feel hectored, as if the author is nagging them to agree.

Indeed, the characters in this excerpt hardly seem real. The lack of specific detail makes them a standard-issue dysfunctional family. But if we'd witnessed a petty argument about deckchairs, we'd be agreeing the pair were unreasonable and stubborn – but making up our own mind.

Note that you don't need to make the passage into a scene. 'Show not tell' doesn't mean 'expand it'. Two lines of well-chosen detail will do fine:

> *Every time she spoke he talked over her. The atmosphere got worse and worse.*

Showing will persuade the reader more effectively than telling.

For your toolbox

✏ Every writer struggles to show not tell, especially if they're fleshing out scenes from notes. Stick a note on your monitor. 'Don't tell; show us HOW.'

✏ Watch out for instances where you're telling the reader what to think of your characters. Instead, give persuasive details so they form that opinion for themselves.

2 Why plots happen: motivation, need and conflict

Stories are about what people do, but they're also about why. So our characters need strong motivations – especially when they cause turmoil and heartache.

A character's actions should be plausible and consistent, even while they are surprising. Often I see manuscripts where characters do things that are hard to believe, but this is usually because the motivations don't make sense. Nothing will stretch credibility if it seems to have a cause. Motivation may be conscious or unconscious. It may come from personality;

perhaps the character can't control their urges. Motivation will also be particular to the individual, a unique cocktail of their personality, history, beliefs and circumstances.

This probably sounds theoretical and vague, but it should become clear in the next section, where I'll discuss what makes characters individual and how that creates a story. For now, here are some general principles.

Dramatic need

Motivation comes from a dramatic need. So a detective needs to solve a murder. A tycoon must protect his family. People in a nuclear war need to stay alive and healthy. A cheating wife must avoid being caught with her lover.

Perhaps the character's need is an emotional hole. The orphan wants to find a family or a long-lost twin. The widow needs to grieve and move on.

In movies, the story is usually constructed around a character's mission to fulfil their dramatic need. Many novels do this too, but they don't have to be so straightforward. Novels are a more interior medium than film; we can explore the characters' inner lives or a poetically hued world. A dramatic need can be used more inventively and intimately. The character may need to suppress or control something while they go about normal life. It may be a question that keeps them in constant unease, oversensitive to other events.

Harriet Vane in *Gaudy Night* by Dorothy L Sayers must decide whether to marry Lord Peter Wimsey. She finds herself investigating a blackmail situation, and it keeps confronting her with this question she simply cannot answer.

Whatever you do with a dramatic need, it should be impossible for the character to ignore. It should drive them to seek an answer — which will give the story purpose.

That journey shouldn't be easy or it won't make much of a story. This is where conflict comes in.

Conflict — a quick guide

Conflict is another vast subject that can fill entire books. Conflict adds complications and keeps the reader interested. On the smallest scale, conflicts in dialogue will keep a scene surprising, human and fresh (I'll talk about dialogue in its own section). On a story scale, conflict creates dilemmas and puts a character into a state of disturbance and instability.

The simplest conflict is the impossible choice. Your protagonist wants to trail a criminal but must avoid the people who want to kill him. He wants to rescue the innocent friend but he will lose his chance to thwart the baddie. He can't do both and yet he must.

These are plot conflicts, imposed by circumstances. Interesting characters also need conflicts that are emotional. They fall in love with someone from the enemy side. They are forced to partner a rival. Maybe the conflict is in their soul — they regret a past deed and are made to examine or even repeat it.

Emotional conflicts will torment the character to their very depths, push them to behave in ways that are not always under their control. They discover their hidden selves and might be changed.

Even if your plot is packed with murders, natural disasters, wars, oppressive political regimes, terrorist uprisings or the world ending, you can use emotional conflict to enrich the characters and keep the reader guessing. Emotional conflicts push a reader's buttons, no matter how alien the situation. They put the story's events into a context that has real meaning This makes them feel for a character and fascinated to know what they will do.

Conflict isn't nice. It requires a writer to get sadistic. I've often thought that if I had to endure the trials I inflict on my characters I'd be a nervous wreck. I blithely make them confront their worst fears. I rope them to companions who will make a situation intolerable. I find their fault lines and jemmy them relentlessly. It's wicked to wish that on people in real life, but absolutely right for stories.

Again, this principle will be revisited throughout the book. If you get good at spotting potential for conflict you'll have character − and story − ideas for ever.

A simple idea + emotional conflict = a story

Much conflict can be found in the simplest situation if you inflict it on the right character. In Margaret Drabble's novel *The Millstone*, a woman finds herself pregnant. Some characters might embrace motherhood. For Drabble's protagonist, it's far from straightforward. The year is 1965 and this lady's an unmarried academic. A hasty marriage isn't out of the question, as the father seems sweet and decent. But she doesn't even tell him. She's torn between terminating the pregnancy and keeping it. Every time she decides on one course, she's pulled the other way. As she goes on, she confronts her feelings about her own childhood, her hopes for her life and the kind of person she thinks she is.

Notice how conflict is particular to this character. Nobody else would get in this mess. Whether your plot comes from external challenges or internal struggles, the principle is the same. Create the individual who will be most tormented and you have a riveting central character.

Really good conflicts put a character into a situation of intolerable strain. Jane Eyre has looked for love all her life and finally finds it in Mr Rochester. But she can only be with him if she is his mistress and loses her hard-won social status, a terrible compromise. What can she do?

Emotional conflicts trap a character in a hideous tug of war. They provide motivations for what might seem like mysterious decisions. Conflicts create a battle in the character's soul, add tension and suspense and transform almost any situation into a long, messy ordeal.

Don't forget supporting characters

Opportunities for conflict are everywhere, and that includes supporting characters. When the protagonists seem to have it too easy, I encourage writers to add conflict from minor characters.

Minor characters can seem lifeless, as though they were staff employed to make a plot run smoothly. But if your hero needs information, send them to the minor character who doesn't want to tell him. If he needs a favour, ask the guy who will take offence.

Small-scale conflicts can make your minor characters complex and real. The science fiction and fantasy writer Jack Vance is masterful at this. His novels are full of crafty, selfish, stubborn or unexpectedly generous individuals with agendas that don't fit those of the main characters. More about minor characters in their own section.

For your toolbox

✐ Individual nature, need and conflict: you'll see them mentioned a lot in this book. Treat them as high-voltage words. They make story puppets into people.

✐ Use dramatic needs to give your characters a problem they can't ignore.

✐ Use conflicts to give your characters dilemmas, drive, desire and desperation.

✐ Conflict is particular to a person. If you think of an interesting plot situation, don't inflict it on an 'average' person. Create a character who will find it exquisitely difficult.

- Make use of minor characters by giving them their own opinions and quirks.

- Like archaeological relics, conflict is everywhere, waiting to be discovered. We just have to keep our eyes open and dig.

3 Fictional people are individuals

Who are your characters? How will the reader bond with their humanity? Are they everyman or everywoman, thrown into a situation we recognise with a cold jolt, because there but for the grace...

Perhaps they are a happy family whose daughter goes missing; the wife whose husband is arrested for murder. Or are your characters called to adventure, for which they have to rise to extraordinary challenges? Perhaps a quest to save the world, or a simple need to survive in a strange environment?

Are they more complex, with unusual depths? The plot might arise because they have a peculiar and intriguing imbalance. They've been living on a tightrope but either didn't realise or managed to muddle through. The story pitches them into crisis, threatening to unravel them. They usually try to put things back as they were, which causes a worse mess. And on they go until the only escape is to face the deepest problem.

However simple or complex you want your characters, they must be believable and individual. This section will deal with the ways that goes wrong and how to fix it.

What the writer intended and what came out on the page

Characters are often real in the writer's mind but not in the reader's. How do we bridge that gulf?

When I critique a manuscript, I ask clients to give me a synopsis as well. I don't read it until I've finished the novel, but I often find vast mismatches between the writer's view of the characters and what comes off the page.

Typically it looks like this. The synopsis says the main character is 'feisty'. But in the scenes that establish her, she waits for emails that don't arrive, thinks about the job she hates, takes phone calls from friends who are cancelling lunch, and goes to Pilates classes.

The writer usually replies: 'But doesn't that tell you she's feisty? She's had a frustrating day.' Um, no. I see a character who has endured a bunch of irritating things. What's more, she does it with barely a murmur. Not the slightest nanograin of feist.

A key piece is missing – the character's reaction.

It's common for writers to think they've demonstrated character when they haven't. To them, the character feels feisty while they're writing her. They know how she reacted and the reason she did things. The iceberg has great depths – but the writer has not shown they exist.

Sometimes the writer is being too subtle. They're asking the reader: imagine all that happened to you. That's a dodgy strategy. We want to see how a character feels, and that is not necessarily the way you or I feel.

The writer who omits these details is often imagining their own reaction, assuming it will be everyone's. This is not even true in the real world, let alone fiction. We all react differently to cancelled lunch meetings etc, according to our personality, how we feel about the friend and what other commitments we have to juggle. Indeed, some characters define themselves by doing what the average reader wouldn't. But even if the character is 'everymanwoman', we need their reaction. If the character doesn't react we draw a conclusion: what happened did not matter. (And no feistiness or frustration are demonstrated at all.)

Later in a story, once we know a character, these blanks work differently. We can supply the reaction. Indeed we react on the character's behalf, an intimacy that increases our connection with them. But in the establishing scenes, it's risky to let us guess. Is the character heroically tolerant or a wimp? Both explanations fit. (This particular excerpt raises more issues, which I'll discuss later – see the difficulties of discontented characters on page 181 and passive central characters on page 73.)

If you show us scenes that define a character, include the character's reaction. That's what tells us who they are.

Character's dramatic need is glossed over in generalisations

Sometimes authors can be too subtle with their protagonist's dramatic need.

I critiqued a manuscript about an adoptee searching for her birth parents. That's a glorious situation, suggesting thousands of ways she might feel different, alone and special. We are curious to see them. They have formed who she is, given her an unusual perspective that will bond us to her. But this is what the writer gave us:

> I'm trying to trace my birth parents. I have always been full of questions.

Is that all? The synopsis confirmed this would be a major issue, but the text never delved further. The writer told me she assumed, by writing those few lines, that readers would understand what the character meant. No more was needed. Those words would convey the weight of the problem like a magic spell.

Like the example in the previous section, this is assuming a generic response when what matters is the specific. What's it like to wonder where you came from? Do you look at families who physically resemble each other and wonder who you're like? Do you feel guilty in case you hurt the family who brought you up? Or do you feel you never belonged with them?

The reader doesn't want to supply those details. They want the writer to; that's why they love stories.

This is one of the times we must mutter 'show not tell'. The character was full of questions: what were they? They won't be the same for everyone. How has this individual been affected by this knowledge? What does she think might happen if she does find her birth parents?

Another manuscript I critiqued understood this principle very well. The main characters were a couple whose child had died in an accident. Even though we'd all agree this is horrifying, the author never left the reader to fill the gaps. He showed us what the death had taken away. How the mother had been enthralled by the child and the husband had watched bemused, not wanting to admit he felt excluded. Then one afternoon he'd taken his daughter for a walk and been overwhelmed by her wide-open smile. The writer also reminded us of the loss in an ordinary conversational remark, or an awkward glance when a friend worried they'd said something tactless. Even though any fool could guess that losing a child would be a tragedy, this author bedded the tragedy into the characters' lives. This made the loss – and them – real.

The big issues of a character's life are personal. The reader can't fill them in from an identikit assumption. And they don't want to.

Besides, real characters do not have 'typical' reactions. There are a million different ways to feel about losses, regrets, puzzles and threats. That also goes for attitudes to parents, spouses, grandchildren, friends, ex-lovers, pets, sports, art. Children are not all cherished angels – consider the skewed parent-child dynamic in Lionel Shriver's *We Need To Talk About Kevin*. Fiction is about the particular, not the generic and 'ordinary'. Look at the pregnant lady in *The Millstone*. Her individual reaction to motherhood made a whole plot.

If a character has a dramatic need, show us what it means to them personally.

No internal life – empty or enigmatic?

Characters grab the reader more if we understand what matters to them, and how the events of the story will make them happy or upset. You might have one main protagonist and show us their thoughts and feelings up close. You might hopscotch between several. But some writers leave out an important character's internal life, hoping to create an enigma. That can just as easily create a sterile read.

Enigmatic characters don't give much away, but they aren't blanks. The trick is to demonstrate an internal life, but not plug the reader into it. Show they have a lively consciousness that responds to events and people, but never go into their heads to reveal their feelings or perspective. The reader will wonder what lies in the depths because they have seen a far-off glimmer that intrigues.

Another approach is to write a character who can channel the reader's curiosity. A Doctor Watson is the human conduit between us and the self-contained, brilliant Sherlock Holmes.

How subtle should you be about your enigma's feelings? Often you can't tell by yourself. It's a question for your test readers or critique group.

Another way writers try to generate mystery is by under-drawing a character. They skimp on background or fail to give them a life beyond their story role (more on that later). This doesn't make a character mysterious; it makes them look inadequately realised. Mystery comes from contradictions, from details that don't add up. It comes from gaps that intrigue. Writers often think that if they leave a character's background or characterisation vague, the reader will fill the blanks. As we've already discussed, blanks must be handled with care. Readers won't fill them unless they are provoked to.

Enigmatic characters work better if they have a background that vibrates with mystery. Try conundrums such as dates that don't match, places that don't exist, former partners who say they have never heard of them. Enigmatic characters must be created actively. Otherwise, the reader might not notice them at all.

Create your enigmatic characters with contradictions that tempt the reader to speculate about the truth.

Writer feels out of their depth with that character or situation

I sometimes see a writer hold back with a significant character, as if wary of writing them with depth. Compared with the other characters, they lack internal life – even the flashes that create an enigma. They also lack the human flaws that the other characters have. It's as if the writer has erected a barrier: not to be explored.

For some reason, the writer feels unable to connect with the character. Perhaps they're a villain (more on villains later), the opposite gender (more on that later too), a different sexual persuasion, or from an unfamiliar social milieu. Maybe these characters have had experiences the writer cannot fathom (although writers are usually excellent at filling the experience gap with research and imagination). This lack of confidence produces a character who is unconvincing and written at arm's length. So how do you connect?

Return to basics. Every significant character wants something. They'll probably also fear something. These needs and anxieties are not very different from yours and mine: they have people they want to protect, roles to fulfil, worries about the future, regrets from the past. You can write almost anybody if you build with those fundamentals.

In your research, set your radar to spot how these might play out in your character's special circumstances. Also, take a look at the exercises section of this book, where I have a game to help you wriggle inside characters who aren't necessarily similar to you. (see page 163).

If you have trouble connecting to a character, find out what matters to them.

Males, females and culture

Some writers and readers worry that men can't create convincing females. The opposite direction doesn't seem to be debated as much, although logic dictates it should be just as tricky. As we're all stuck with one or other chromosome set, what are we to do if we want to write a significant character who is the opposite of us?

This is very much a question of personal style and genre. Women who write for male audiences often adopt a masculine-looking pen name or are given one by their publisher. Are they ever unmasked or does the cover name prevent readers wondering about the writer's true gender? For some writers, gender authenticity never becomes an issue. It might not be a burning concern in the story. Or perhaps the writer pulls it off with innate sense. This is hardly unlikely – after all, we spend many years reading the written output of both genders.

I had first-person narrators of both genders in *My Memories of a Future Life*, and found myself thinking a different way for each. There were no specific tricks I can pinpoint; I wrote what felt right for the personality. Reviewers seemed convinced, but did the personality make the gender or the gender make the personality? Who knows.

And obviously the character's personality is important. The world is full of women who aren't feminine and men who are.

Good fiction is full of people who are unusual. Some genres won't like those expectations to be subverted, though, especially in main characters. You need to judge what fits your genre and story.

Also consider the historical and cultural situation. In the developed world, twenty-first century men and women live similar lives. In the nineteenth century, a woman might faint if given a shock. But was that because women were protected from shocks or because society expected it? By the time we get to the twenty-first century, we can't imagine any female fainting from shock.

When Hilary Mantel recreates Tudor England in *Wolf Hall* and *Bring Up the Bodies*, female characters might be referred to by their father's name: Sir John Seymour's girl; Thomas Boleyn's girl. Fantasy authors often create societies like our historical periods, but forget how culture influences their characters' lives. They base a female on their cousin who lives on the West Coast right now – who behaves in a 21st century way. Your woman must not only be a woman, but a woman of her time, with the corresponding attitudes about morality, ambition, religion and science. (And so must the men.) Don't forget the physical environment. Attitudes to pain, comfort, hunger, heat, cold, clothing, laundry, education, sanitation, hygiene, disease and death all shift with the time and culture.

Professions and life roles also influence a character's vocabulary, preoccupations and thoughts. A female doctor doesn't talk the same as a full-time mother, even though both are women. More on that in the section on dialogue.

But sometimes critique partners and editors tell us we've got it wrong. Our girl is blokish or the guy feels girly. What's making them think that? And what should we do?

Fantasy author Livia Blackburne had an interesting experience when her husband read a scene she'd written that featured two 17-year-old friends. She's given me permission to quote their conversation:

'Let me get this straight. Jack falls off his horse.' Husband jabbed his finger at my draft. 'Why isn't Tristam laughing?'

I blinked. 'What?'

'He should be laughing his head off. You know how mean 17-year-old boys are to each other?'

'But falling off a horse is serious! Wouldn't Tristam be worried about Jack being hurt?'

Husband gave me a long-suffering look. 'If Jack's breathing, and conscious, Tristam should be laughing.'

Poor Livia had misjudged guy conversation too.

'And this passage here.' Husband read it out. ' "You fell off your horse?" asked Tristam. The question came out more incredulously than intended and Tristam wondered whether Jack would be offended or pleased at his tone."' Husband raised his eyebrows. 'You have a dude, thinking about what another dude is feeling? About the tone of his voice?'

Unconvinced, and a tad dismayed, Livia showed the passage to various male friends. Would they split their sides when a pal fell off a horse? Most of them admitted they would.

When you read about gender differences, the consensus is that men like to talk about problems and solutions. To use Livia's example: Jack took a pratfall and his male friends thought this was hilarious. If his friends had been female, they would have examined his feelings and given him sympathy. These distinctions are still a product of society, though. Men in a formal respect-based culture might be more concerned with loss of face. This is a question to consider when you create your world.

Can we be more scientific? Yes we can.

In 2003 a team of Israeli scientists devised an experiment to predict whether a document was written by a man or a woman. After analysing 600 pieces of writing, they came up with an algorithm, the Gender Genie, that was 80% accurate – or a lot more reliable than the flip of a coin. They agreed women were more inclined to think in terms of people and relationships, and men about things. But the way they drew this conclusion was interesting.

The Gender Genie disregarded the documents' content, so it made no difference whether the subject was childrearing or car maintenance. Instead it looked at unobtrusive tics. It found women used more personal pronouns – 'I', 'you', 'he' and 'she' especially. They wrote about connections to things – 'my car', 'your dog', 'their house'. Men preferred 'a', 'the', 'that' and 'these', plus quantifiers like 'more' and 'some'. 'The car, some dogs, a house'. The nouns themselves didn't matter, but the preceding qualifier did.

Authors report that they've used the Gender Genie to nail that elusive XX/XY factor – especially when test readers have complained the voice didn't sound right. They've revised manuscripts with those principles and satisfied their editors – and crucially never mentioned they were using a 'magic formula'.

So if you're in difficulties, the Gender Genie seems to be helpful. But don't forget the characters also have to make sense in their historical and cultural context. Sixteenth-century girls, no matter how intelligent or enlightened, don't look authentic if they have the concerns of twenty-first-century grrls.

Characters have no life outside the plot

Some characters don't do or think about anything except the plot events. They never mention anyone besides the characters we see.

If one or a few characters have a narrow life, that's interesting. That tells us something about them. But if no characters seem to belong to a wider world, it looks weird.

Characters need other things in their lives besides the central plot situation. Often writers forget to show these. Maybe they haven't thought about them. Or they fear they are irrelevant or too ordinary.

But real people have a web of commitments and routines − school, jobs, family, friends, hobbies, abandoned projects or interests, things they intend to get round to. They usually have romantic relationships, or are noted not to have them. Sure, these aren't all germane to the central plot question. But if a character lacks them, they appear to go into suspended animation until it's time to play a scene.

Furthermore, your characters' routines have to convince. They must create structure in the character's day or week. If there's a job and family, the character must prioritise them, which may clash with the demands of the plot. I frequently see characters who refer to work commitments, then abandon all obligations as the story heats up.

It takes a bit more sweat to invent this, but once you do it's surprising how alive the characters feel. This extra life context can also feed back into the plot or themes, suggesting new alleys for the story to explore. It might create interesting obstacles. If Fiona gets a black eye, what will her colleagues at the solicitor's office say? If she's a lady's maid, what will her mistress's reaction be?

Even if the characters are confined in a limiting location, such as a space station or an ocean-going ship, they need downtime. They must talk about – and do – things that are not their plot role. If they are wedded to their work, they will still have worries, fears, likes and dislikes, most embarrassing moments.

Certain attitudes will mark them out as individuals: team members they can't stand; others they feel comfortable with.

Communities who are brought together by work usually have a gossip network, because they need to form alliances and create their own territories.

Give the characters a life beyond the central problem of the story.

Too much trivial detail

Here's the flipside. Sometimes writers clutter the story with too much of this background. We get scene upon scene of character downtime; each conversation word for word; every beat of inconsequential action. This can be exhausting for the reader. They'll grasp quite quickly that the character has a life, and will scrutinise the detail for an additional underlying point. They might also decide your characters aren't going to do anything. (That may suit your purposes. If not, read on.)

One of my clients wrote a long scene about her protagonist spending a quiet evening at home. It was several pages of inconsequential phone calls. Brenda called and the character talked to her. Then her stepfather; then a colleague, then the residents' association. What did they say? Nothing much. It was just humans catching up.

It was certainly realistic, but the reader would be overwhelmed. They would be trying to keep track of everyone – she has an Auntie, Mum, Bizzy the cat-sitter, Pete the friend, Steve the other friend. He said this, she said that. They talked about someone called Paul, or was it Pauline? Who the blazes is Brenda?

This is fine if it's important to make the reader ask those

questions. They might advance the plot or echo the theme. But if they are only there for atmosphere, we need to treat the material differently.

The client and I reframed the scene, considering what the reader had to take away. There was nothing to learn from the dialogue, and it didn't matter who called. But we wanted to create the impression that the character was busy and had friends. If this scene was a photographic composition, these callers might be shown in the background, maybe out of focus. They would add depth but wouldn't distract from the important subject. So instead of showing the conversations in real time, we could shrink them to a summary. In the end, it worked best to turn them into messages, with the protagonist's reactions:

> *Brenda called. She'll want to talk about Fred but I'm too tired for that right now. Stepfather − darn, I was going to give him the number of that insurance company. Steve from the Swindon office − can't it wait until after the weekend? The residents' association – yes I'd said I'd help with the posters for the garage sale. Can I get away with not calling back until tomorrow?*

That thicket of trivial talk shrank to one paragraph. We now had a character with an authentic life. It could sketch some of her routines and obligations and the people she might talk about, but it wasn't given undue prominence. Indeed, it would be better included as texture in a scene where something more significant was happening. (Scenes that have more than one function keep a story moving and are more satisfying than scenes that merely sketch background.)

The same goes for characters with interesting pasts. You don't have to tell us every detail. Indeed, if you pay out background in glimpses, you can create more depth because you let the reader use intuition.

In *Wolf Hall*, Hilary Mantel makes veiled references to Thomas Cromwell's roguish past before he comes to King Henry's court. She hints that he might have killed a man. Other characters occasionally refer to it as a rumour. Cromwell himself dwells on an unclear memory fragment. Later in the book he teaches his sons a blow that can kill and we wonder where that knowledge came from. But we never get a 'reveal' scene to explain. It remains shady, to build Cromwell's reputation, ruthlessness and physical presence – for the other characters and also for the reader. Cromwell also suspects he may have fathered children in those lost years. This starts to trouble him as his own children mature, and his older self feels he would like to know these unknown others.

Mantel might have brought this background forwards, but she keeps it as glimpses. This creates a curious and appealing vulnerability, making Cromwell a man with a human centre. Glimpsed details can make a character more real and true.

Of course, you may add detail for deliberate effect. Stieg Larsson begins *The Girl With The Dragon Tattoo* with a character who receives mysterious pictures of flowers every year. Everything stops for a leisurely discourse on the kinds of bloom and where they grow, as though we were touring the book's world with a magnifying glass.

This eases us into the mindset of a detective, who can't allow any observation to pass without evaluating and classifying it.

Background detail – and indeed back story – should be used with care. Too little and the characters act in a peculiar void. Too much, and the story is suffocated. But you can also create inventive effects according to the way you defocus, hint, expand and condense.

Describing characters – too much physical detail

On the subject of too much, some writers hit us with a top-to-toe description the first time we meet a character.

This is not usually necessary unless there is a compelling reason for the reader – or narrator character – to be interested in the character's appearance. We understand the world stops when you meet the President of the United States or a long-lost daughter. Or if you zip back in time to find yourself thrillingly nose to nose with Cleopatra. Otherwise, though, all that description holds up the flow. Why? Because the reader isn't ready to absorb it.

It's best to tantalise with just a few details. And don't confine it to visuals.

Really good descriptions give us a sense of what it's like to be in a room with a character. Here's John le Carre and *A Small Town in Germany*:

> *Bradfield was a hard-built, self-denying man, thin-boned and*

well preserved, of that age and generation which can do with very little sleep.

Newspaper obituaries can teach us a lot about describing characters. They often feature people the reader has never met, which is exactly what novelists do. Obituarists don't rely on visual details. Blue eyes and a crooked front tooth don't mean much if the reader doesn't already have a mental picture.

Obituarists concentrate on summoning the subject's presence with their habits and expressions. I still remember an obit I read many years ago about an eminent female chemist who always had a worried expression, as though she feared a catastrophe was happening in the next room. I've long forgotten her name or what she did (alas), but I still know what it would be like to spend time with her. Another obit I still remember was about a religious leader who had the disconcerting habit of closing his eyes while he spoke.

Another point about descriptions: make sure that on subsequent meetings we'll know it's the same person. Include a distinguishing detail that always recurs, such as glasses at a wonky angle or an elaborate ring the character wears. It needn't be visual: perhaps a rasping cough or a smell of patchouli. Use this to announce the character, then drop in other details to reveal their appearance gradually. (Does this ring a bell? It's show, not tell.)

You don't have to describe the character top to toe on first meeting. Use short, vivid impressions to put us in their presence, and add to the reader's mental picture each time they appear.

Please, not like a famous person

Some writers try to describe a character by reference to a famous person from movies, public life or even another novel. This is fine if the narrative voice is a character, but usually looks lazy in a neutral, third-person manuscript. And even if you are writing as a character, the comparison with the famous person is not as effective as a description of your own.

She was as fat as John Belushi

is not as interesting as

Her neck was so plump it gave her the look of a face painted on a thumb.

Looking in the mirror: awkward reasons for characters to ponder their appearance

Here's a peculiar thing writers do. They make a character think about their appearance so they can tell us about it. This is usually performed while dressing and may involve a mirror. It's often, but not always, a feature of stories written in first person.

There's nothing intrinsically wrong with those two actions. What's wrong is when the character describes things they don't have a reason to remark on.

In *The Slap* by Christos Tsiolkas, many of the characters are inclined to gaze at their reflection or a body part and think about their lives. This looks stagey and artificial. And even more so because the novel has eight narrators and most of them do it.

While we might accept that one character has an odd habit, we can't accept that eight will (except as a clue to something).

Contrast this with Ruth Rendell's novel *The Keys To The Street*, which also has a number of point-of-view characters. We never see them in the mirror. Indeed we might have only the sketchiest idea of what they look like, but we still know their situations and inner lives. These are revealed in diverse ways and aren't manufactured so the characters can think for the reader's benefit. They are activities from the characters' usual routine. The dog walker collects his animals and does his job, meanwhile plotting and fulminating − which lets us into his world. The violent psychotic takes crack and demonstrates his worst impulses. The tragic down-and-out goes for epic walks, considering his life while he pushes the barrow that contains his possessions.

But sometimes you might find good reasons to introduce a character with a deliberate, staged 'think'. Perhaps they have a reason to take stock. Even getting dressed can look fresh if they have reason to pay special attention. Perhaps it's their wedding day. Or the last day with two breasts before a mastectomy. With that, all contrivance vanishes.

Sometimes you can take the bull by the horns. If your character knows they are the narrator of a book, they might have a plausible reason to describe themselves.

I work hard at a job that I couldn't have imagined tolerating at school when I was a stagestruck wannabe actress. My hair's neat and short – I doubt the people who gave me the 1985 Bad Hair Award would recognise me now. I thought I'd be the kind of person who'd find themselves writing their memoir but I assumed it would be after a long, glittering life. I might even have thought someone else would write it for me. Such are the expectations of callow youth. Where did my ambitious self go? I look a bit different now from that pierced, shock-haired, fame-dreaming Goth.

(Notice how the character's appearance is really a way of demonstrating change and hinting at a journey. It's not just about how she looks.)

If the character has to think about their appearance, find a good reason. Then have fun with it.

A carnival of odd misfits – tics and physical characteristics are not character

In their quest to make characters distinctive, some writers go too far. They give their characters tics, peculiar speech habits and outlandish wardrobes. Sometimes I think they're imagining how eye-catching their cast will look when listed on the dust-jacket – a 25-stone fitness instructor, her one-legged best friend, her anorexic flatmate, the family home with the ruined abattoir out back. They are striving to create an interesting, quirky world but it's more like a freak show.

Although these externals might look exciting, they are not character. Character is internal – the person's agendas and attitudes. Characters need to be distinctive on the inside, not the outside.

Having said that, misfits make intriguing characters. But that's because of how they feel and the way people treat them. If they are so strange, what problems does it give them? How do their personalities make that easier or harder? If you have a bunch of misfits who hang out in a group, what binds them together? How do they cope with life challenges? What ordinary things do they do? When do they encounter people who aren't like them, and what happens?

Those peculiarities might not be visible. A character may look as normal as an onion, but have impulses they would never confess, even to a close friend. They might suppress parts of themselves because of pride, obligations or what is socially acceptable.

These worries, needs and desires might make the character feel isolated, because they churn away with no relief. Perhaps the character isn't fully aware of their most fundamental agenda.

That's the true depth of the misfit story. It can provide the profoundest reward if the feeling is eased.

But does every 'misfit' story have to end with the character's difference 'cured'? Not at all.

How often in fiction has a character said 'I can't change who I am'? As a line it's trite, but it's nevertheless true. The misfit characteristic may be too deeply bedded for a solution. Although you can put this character in a story that uncovers their nature, it might not end with their change. People and events might change around them. They might adjust to a new equilibrium. But the characteristic could be mysterious and immutable − a symptom of the human condition, a question with no answer because life isn't like that. The choice is yours.

Great misfit characters are not just different on the outside. Find out how they are peculiar in their soul.

Teenagers

Speaking of misfits, what about teenagers? I see a lot of misguided attempts to create main characters in their teens. Writers give them short tempers, rebellious natures, outrageous clothes, faddy crazes, ferociously held beliefs, untidy bedrooms, unusual sleeping patterns and peculiar slangy vocabulary.

These certainly are teen characteristics, but they are not a personality. If you create a teen character using only these behaviours, you risk creating a caricature.

Of course, teens are different from kids and adults. Brain geeks have found that from the age of 10 our grey matter gets a massive reshuffle. Add hormones and you have a volatile creature indeed. But this doesn't create a person; it adjusts one who already exists.

So I find it more helpful to create teenagers in the same way as any character.

Find their core personality and work out where they fit (or don't). Pay particular attention to the emotional environment, particularly family. What attitudes prevail at home and how do they shape your character? What's their culture? Are they in an ethnic minority, and therefore not like others?

Birth order can make a difference to the way the character is treated and how they feel. Is your teen an only child, second child, middle child, much younger or older, the only girl?

Are the parents divorced or in an unusual arrangement? Where do these create conflict with the character's nature and hopes?

How happy is the character?

Once you've found the person your character has always been, you can magnify, diminish (or rewire) with a dash of teen spirit. Each individual will develop at their own rate, so here's a very rough and averaged guide.

Lack of concentration At about age 10, kids aren't good at evaluating how well they're doing a task, leaning from experience and staying focused on something difficult. They might have trouble remembering lists of instructions, which may exasperate teachers and parents. By age 15, they are as good as adults if motivated, but scatterbrained if not. By 16, they are good at problem-solving and at 20 they are as responsible, conscientious and applied as older adults.

Mood swings Teens have to deal with a changing body and an upgrading brain. Stress and tiredness can make them vile-tempered, even though at other times they might be easy-going or enthusiastic. This may be baffling to everyone else. It starts at age 11, when they can be exuberant one minute and angry or tearful the next. Withdrawal and anxiety usually peaks at age 13 (generally regarded as the moodiest year). By 15 they are less emotional and expressive, though inside they may be unhappy, introverted and thoughtful. With moods being so unstable, they usually find it hard to resist temptation. They often can't stop themselves before they make a mistake or a tactless remark. Most of the changes have finished by 16, when they become better at controlling their impulses. They also become more considerate and empathetic.

Risk-taking Teenhood is obviously an age of rebellion. Adolescents seek the unusual, the unexpected and the thrilling. They think they are old enough to handle risky situations and will be scornful when adults tell them they're not. At age 12, it's credible for a few to start trying drugs, cigarettes or alcohol. Rebellion peaks at around 15. By 17 they might have a driving licence and many of them will drive too fast. Under-25s have the highest accidental death rate — most of us have known of a teen who came to grief in a fast car. But not all teens are risk-takers. Some might establish their independence by refusing to copy others' idiotic behaviour. The adventurous characteristic will spur most teens to seek new people, so your adolescent character might dare to join groups or situations an adult wouldn't approach.

Sex By 12, boys and girls are interested in each other but girls seek out boys more actively. By 15, it's likely that many will be sexually active. By 16, most will be dating and many will have regular sex. By 17, intimacy and soul mates become important, although guys will still be emotionally immature and girls may be vulnerable.

Clothes and money Image and grooming become important at 12 or 13. Money too, and a lot of mid-teenagers are broke. By around 16, many will have a part-time job and can handle responsibility.

Family At age 10, most kids are respectful of authority. At 11 they generally get rebellious. They'll treat their friends better than those they live with, be competitive with siblings and critical of parents, but by 12 this reaction to family calms down. Privacy starts to be important at about 13, and this is the age when parents are perceived as embarrassing and nagging. Different relationships may form with father and mother. Toys have been outgrown, but girls may still hang onto teddy bears.

Friends As family becomes irksome at 11, close friends become significant. Teens like to belong to a peer group and find them more stimulating and relevant than same-old family. From this age on, they become aware of the future, that they will one day make their lives with people they have chosen. By 13, boys tend to hang out in groups. Girls prefer smaller groups – typically three, with two who are close and another who is the outsider. At 14, friendships may be forming and dissolving rapidly, then patching up again. If a friendship dies or the character is excluded from a party, it feels catastrophic. By 16, the make and break is not so frenetic. Sixteen-year-olds are more self-sufficient, more sensitive towards others and friendly.

Humour and sarcasm Kids start to develop a strong sense of humour by about 12, and discover sarcasm and double meanings. By 13, they're likely to be mocking family and teachers. By 16 the sense of humour is more adult and less cruel.

Ethics and the outside world A sense of ethics and justice tends to start at 11. By 13, teens often have a sophisticated understanding of world issues and a moral sense. By 16, they are keen to find new ideas, new people and new ways of doing things. They might also be acquiring a vocation. As with adult characters, be aware of what drives your teens, impresses them, enrages them, inspires or annoys.

Art, music, movies and books Age 12, your characters will probably like entertainment that gives them heroes and role models. Age 13, they seek characters like themselves, with similar relationships and issues. By about 16, they are less self-obsessed and enjoy sitcoms, reality shows, soap operas, game shows, MTV, social and political issues, romantic comedies and social drama. By 17, many will graduate from teen music and books and explore adult culture.

Pressure and change The pressure that teens feel is often overwhelming. Not only are they dealing with physical changes, their worlds are in immense upheaval. Obviously, schoolwork becomes important like never before, but the changes go further than that. Family and friends, even if not ideal, used to stand for the steady and reliable. In the teenage years, they become sources of stress, hassle and worry, and often also conflict.

A final point about teens is inexperience. In this, they aren't much different from any other character, as most novels feature people who are thrown into challenging situations. With teens, though, their inexperience presents a bigger canvas.

Also, they are more likely to test boundaries, be optimistic and seek new thrills. So treat them as any other character who finds themselves tempted, scared, bewildered, liberated, hurt and healed by a strange world.

What do they hide, even if they are 'normal'? Rounded characters and the double life of Isobel

Life is complex and many of us wear different masks. And so might your major characters.

As I walked to the Tube one morning I saw a card on the pavement, dropped from a gift. It said *Dear Isobel, Happy birthday! With love from Izzy xxx* An amusing duality, and obviously she didn't write it to herself.

But it made me think how people aren't the same all the time, with everyone.

Among friends, somebody might be fizzy Izzy. At work she might conquer the world with the stern face of Isobel. Or maybe she is well-behaved Isobel to her family, with her long hair constrained in a neat bun. Elsewhere she lets it down as Izzy.

Colleagues don't know what we're like under the professional mask. Close friends don't know the personality we adopt to do our duty – perhaps fighting fires, standing up in court to prosecute a thief, ruling the kingdom. Children don't realise their parents are so interesting, and parents don't realise their children are so curious, inventive or independent.

A three-dimensional character has different sides – even if they think they don't have much to hide, and even to people who see them all the time.

Imagine Isobel's cohorts wrote a list of what they know about her. Would that match a list made by Izzy's gang? When is this character Izzy and when is she Isobel? How do the two halves dress? What do they talk about? What kind of people do they mix with?

In *Rebecca*, Daphne Du Maurier shows Maxim has a side that the narrator doesn't know. Other characters hint that when Rebecca was alive he was volatile and sparky, but with his new wife he is quiet and mellow. This generates a mystery, of course, and preys on the narrator's insecurities. She feels a very poor substitute for the glittering Rebecca.

Going back to Izzy/Isobel, we can also consider inter-character chemistry. Who brings out Isobel and who brings out Izzy?

The infamous reality TV show *Big Brother* may not have been the most subtle entertainment, but in its early days it was a lab for studying personal chemistry. In the first UK series one housemate looked so shy she was invisible — until one of the other characters left, at which point she magnified. If someone new arrives in the story, it might be like putting a powerful magnet in the room. Might Izzy (or Isobel) suddenly come alive?

Running with this idea, could these two sides be a source of conflict?

Perhaps Isobel works under cover. Or she wants to accept a safe job offer and also yearns to follow her dream. Or maybe Izzy is a junior incarnation while Isobel wants to be taken seriously – Debbie Harry becomes Deborah Harry.

Isobel might not even know she's hiding Izzy. Another UK reality TV series, *Faking It*, used to throw a person into a world they found profoundly awkward. So a young clog dancer from rural Cornwall would be taken to London and made to learn raunchy R&B routines. A classical cellist became a nightclub DJ. A naval officer transformed into a drag queen. They were often horrified by the new world because it broke their personal rules. But bit by bit, they found a new character inside who wanted to be part of it.

This kind of change is immensely satisfying. Could Isobel be liberated to become Izzy? If at the end of the story we found a note from Izzy to Isobel, what would it say?

Explore the many people your characters could be. We'll come back to this later.

Narrator has stranglehold so characters never come alive on their own

Sometimes the writer won't allow characters to speak for themselves.

Here's what it looks like. Have you ever watched an attorney cross-examine a witness in court and felt there was more to know, if only they would let the witness talk?

I often see authors do this. They comment on the characters but don't let them act or speak independently − except to confirm an observation the narrator has made about them.

Of course, that effect may be exactly what you want. Many fine novels are written with 'attorney narrators', whose voice and view are running the show. You can create a fascinating tension between what the narrator says and what is really going on. Think Nabokov and *Lolita*. Another unreliable narrator I like is the manipulative uncle in Andrea Newman's *An Evil Streak*.

These are novels in which the narrator is at least as important as the other characters. In them − and in other stylised narratives such as satire or comedy − it's no problem if the strongest character is the person writing the book. However, I often see attorney narrators when this isn't the intention. The writer wants to present a fully rounded cast, but smothers them with too much direction.

For instance:

> *Susan was the meanest of the four friends. 'I had the cheapest thing on the menu,' she said. 'I think we should each pay our own share.'*

There may be more to know about Susan and her situation. But like a Rottweiler attorney, the narrator doesn't let her tell her side of the story. It makes me imagine a real Susan who's being squashed by the author, like this:

> *Narrator: Did you have the cheapest thing on the menu,*

Susan? Answer yes or no.

Susan: Yes, but –

Narrator: And did you use that as an argument for not sharing the bill equally, as would be considered normal among a group of friends out for a social evening?

Susan: Yes, but –

Narrator: No further questions.

Journalists (and of course lawyers) tend to use attorney narrators. This is because they are taught to write to an agenda rather than explore the nuanced truth. They write scenes that consist of summary and comment, with very little live action to show what anyone is saying or doing. When the characters do act or speak, it is only to confirm the narrator's assertion – like Susan being questioned by the attorney. It is telling us what they are like, rather than showing (I warned you we'd be mentioning that rather often).

The effect of this domineering style is to make the characters look like puppets, not independent people.

So allow your characters to talk back to the attorney. Susan, for instance, might have quite a lot to say:

'I just lost my job and my bathroom ceiling has fallen in. I was going to cancel this evening because I can't afford restaurants like this, but it was your birthday and I wanted you to feel your friends still supported you and weren't taking

sides in your divorce. And you ordered vintage Moet and I'm not drinking because I'm driving, and...'

You see how much she has to say when you let her? Do you see how the character feels she's in the right and how much conflict might arise from this? Characters' personal agendas help make them three-dimensional.

Conversely, you may intend Susan to be mean. How might you show this, instead of telling us? Perhaps her other friends might talk about it:

'I'm dieting,' said Susan. 'I'll pay for my own because I didn't have pudding and wine.'

Beneath the table, Harriet's thumbs were working her phone.

Jeremy's phone vibrated with a message. 'The only diet she's on is the Scrooge plan.'

Although you as the author may know a lot about your characters, they come alive when they speak for themselves.

Characters too similar to each other

Similarity is a two-ended writing weapon. It can create unity, a root note that pulls the narrative elegantly together. So you might explore a theme, such as characters misusing love affairs, family and marriage, but within it you need variation.

If all the characters seem to twist love in the same way it looks as though you couldn't think of more than one permutation.

Even worse, it makes the characters look like mouthpieces for your messages.

Central characters need to be distinct and different. And no, you don't get away with similarity if your characters all belong to the same family. If they share DNA, show it expressed in different ways.

Characters might sound similar because they come from the same culture and social milieu. But even so, there can be variation in the characters' different natures.

In the simplest terms, some would be introvert and some extravert. Some will see the glass as half-full. The emotions and urges behind their speech and thoughts would not be the same.

In Ruth Rendell's novel *The Keys To The Street*, there are several characters who are homeless or nearly homeless, but each has their own internal landscape. Some feel persecuted, some are tragically numbed.

Indeed, characters in the same circles have many reasons not to be similar. They might have an assortment of occupations, which would make them tackle a variety of life problems and people. In some manuscripts, the TV scriptwriter seems just like the doctor, who is identical to the dairy farmer – in a way that doesn't make sense. But in *The Keys To The Street*, the girl who works in the Irene Adler museum is nothing like the former butler who walks everyone's dogs. Their environment and back stories shine through in their attitudes, especially the extent to which they trust other characters. Again, the girl in the museum believes good of people whereas the dog-walker suspects nasty motives in everyone. More on differentiating characters later, in the section on dialogue.

Often, writers don't realise they've created only one character, and it's usually because they haven't thought about them as separate individuals.

This homogenisation is especially likely in stories where a character is fighting society, perhaps trapped in an oppressive regime. The book demands a cast who mostly toe the line. Although the rebel character might be drawn distinctly, the others are duplicates of each other.

The trick is to make them conform in their individual way. In George Orwell's *Nineteen Eighty-Four*, many of the characters obey the party line, but each is different. In just one family he shows this – the children are brutish monsters who pretend to be thought police. Their mother, while law abiding, is terrified of them. Their father is an enthusiastic member of committees that organise community hikes, savings campaigns and spontaneous demonstrations.

Less dystopically, this problem also arises when a main character has friends who mostly appear as a group: a crowd who hang out in the same bar; colleagues in an office; villagers searching for a body. Again, they shouldn't look like clones.

If they're working for a common goal, they could have different ideas of how it should be done. If the story has room this could lead to conflict, or you could keep it as low-key grumbles that provide humour and humanity. You could even use it to suggest there are no easy answers to your major characters' predicament.

Once you know what makes your characters belong together, find what makes them different.

Should you change to a new viewpoint character once the novel is well under way?

I had a client with a very interesting novel who switched his viewpoint character two-thirds through. He had good reasons. The original character had become a terrorist, and the writer feared we would find him too mad and remote. So a new hero was introduced, who was on course to find the terrorist at the end.

It was a clever idea, but flawed. This second character was completely new. We'd never met him or anyone connected to him. We didn't want a new protagonist. Even though our original guy had crossed some unforgivable lines, we'd been with him in gentler times and wanted to continue that contact. If a character was to take his place, he would be competing with our desire to stay with the original one. We'd have to be equally curious about him.

For the reader, it was like starting a new book. Had we met him earlier, perhaps in his own parallel story, we might not feel the loss so much.

Swapping to a new viewpoint character can add fascinating perspective, but only if they're connected to our original people. Barbara Vine (the other side of Ruth Rendell) does this at the end of *No Night Is Too Long*, bringing in the viewpoint of a character who hasn't narrated so far but has been a significant player.

You might have several viewpoint characters, of course. If you do, it's a good idea to establish the pattern early so the reader is primed to switch 'voices' in their heads. If you can't introduce the other narrators until later, create a reason that will make narrative sense, such as a character dying or leaving town, or a diary being found. Barbara Vine prepares us in *No Night Is Too Long* by writing the novel as a memoir interspersed with occasional letters. We're already used to multiple voices, so the new ones blend seamlessly.

When you change viewpoint character you're fighting the reader's resistance. They usually don't want to switch, and might assume the book has given up on the character that was gripping them.

Having said that, there are stories that transfer viewpoint character with curious and unsettling success. Alfred Hitchcock's *Psycho* famously despatches poor Marion Crane and leaves us in the world of her murderer. But he has a strong narrative link with Marion, and becomes a force of evil that replaces her. We aren't left unattached, though. We root for the people who are looking for her. Like us, they are trying to understand what has happened.

If you change viewpoint characters late in the book, prepare the reader to be involved in the new perspective.

Usually your viewpoint character is the person who'll have the most dramatic journey. Here are some less straightforward approaches.

In *Wuthering Heights* the key characters are the lovers, but the story is told by a solicitor and the family servant. They can show us scenes where the lovers aren't present and the ripples caused by their behaviour. The reader is drawn into a neighbourly gossip circle, by turns outraged, disapproving and awestruck. The device also helps bridge a possible plausibility gap by adding a base note of ordinary life and values.

Perhaps your viewpoint character is looking back on childhood. In Michael Frayn's *Spies* a pensioner recalls an episode when he was growing up in World War II. It is his young self who has the most profound change, but the older character adds the poignant distance of years, especially when he revisits the London street and sees how it has changed. We emerge to look at our own neighbourhoods and wonder about vanished stories. His perspective also makes it clear that this is a book for adults, rather than an adventure story for children.

Philip Roth set his novel *Nemesis* in a polio epidemic in New Jersey in 1944. In an interview with the critic Erica Wagner he explained he had a number of possible viewpoints – a parent, a doctor, a survivor looking back. He made his central character a physical education instructor who works with children – a young man called Bucky with new issues of responsibility. One by one, the children he's coaching fall prey to the disease. The novel is narrated by one of the crippled boys, who runs into Bucky some years later. They become friends and Bucky confesses his fears that he was a carrier for the disease, a dialogue that allows them both to seek understanding and closure.

So a viewpoint character need not be the person who is most embroiled in the drama. But they must have their own significant response or perspective.

Characters who are only symbols

Some writers intend one of their central characters to be a symbol, an embodiment of a theme, a nemesis or a complementary dimension of another character. That's fantastic when it works, but...

I see a lot of manuscripts where the symbol character stands out like a wooden actor in an otherwise convincing cast. Their dialogue and behaviour is smothered by the weight of meaning they carry. The writer seems to keep them specially apart, as if to say 'he's a message from me to you about this theme. See how he only says lofty things'.

How do you write a character who has symbolic weight but isn't leaden? You have to persuade the reader to make the comparisons. Meanwhile, you fit the character naturally into the story.

In Thomas Harris's *Red Dragon*, the protagonist is Will Graham, a detective who took early retirement after catching the notorious Hannibal Lecter. Graham is persuaded out of hiding to catch another serial killer, Francis Dolarhide, and has to visit Lecter in jail to enlist his help.

The two murderers past and present are fully fledged characters but they also stand for unresolved aspects of Graham. Hannibal Lecter is his old demons, the horrible instincts that allow him to intuit these murderers' motives and next moves. Indeed Lecter tells Graham:

 'you only caught me because you're just like me'.

On the surface, that's clever, nasty needling. It's also the author nudging us.

Their back stories reinforce these parallels. When Graham tackled Lecter, he didn't conquer him, he locked him away, then locked himself inside a mental breakdown.

Dolarhide, the new murderer, is these demons re-emerging. How does the writer persuade us of this?

Dolarhide is presented in a similar way to Graham. We first see him as monstrous and peculiar, then we see him gentled when he falls in love. Having a girlfriend makes Dolarhide painfully vulnerable. The girl is blind too − which makes us fear for her because she doesn't know his true nature. You could say Graham's wife has a measure of blindness, as she sees (mostly) the family man. Dolarhide is nearly redeemed, but he can't conquer the insecure animal that is also part of his nature, which leads to the traditional do-or-die battle in the climax. And perhaps the only thing that keeps Graham human in this world is that he has a loving wife and a son. *Red Dragon* is a murder story, but Will Graham is also (or maybe really) doing battle with the inhumanity in himself.

So characters who are symbols must work as people first. Mrs Danvers in *Rebecca* represents (among other things) the lonely, bitter voice that reminds the second Mrs de Winter of her social inferiority. But she is also disconcertingly real.

Victor Frankenstein's monster is indisputably real, and he's also the repressed characteristics his creator doesn't want to face.

This type of symbolism is fairly straightforward. It uses character traits and fates that are plausible in the world of the story. More tricky is when you want to suggest a character has a spiritual or supernatural role in a down-to-earth story – for instance, a guardian angel. If it's done too overtly the reader's common sense is likely to reject it.

Again, you have to bury it and offer clues. Tell the story straight and get us involved with the characters and what matters to them. Add a layer of resonance with more subliminal devices – your use of atmosphere, language and theme. Don't forget structure – Thomas Harris's carefully drawn parallels are a good benchmark. Create an exoskeleton around the story that the reader won't see when they're caught up in details and drama, but will understand when they step back and think. Your goal is that when they close the book, they muse to themselves: 'In a way Jasmine is a reincarnation of Justin and fulfilled the potential he was unable to'. They'll also feel ever so satisfied that they worked it out.

Make symbol characters work as people first, and use the structure, language and imagery to make the reader spot the extra significance.

Dystopia problem: characters are dummies to show off the world

Sometimes writers are inspired to create a story because they want to explore a world. An example of this is dystopias with extreme issues, prejudices, unfairnesses and prohibitions.

These issues frequently swamp the characters. So the novel consists of scenes that show segregated schools, no-go zones in the city and third-class compartments on trains. But the characters do very little. They sit in these environments and chat about trivialities, like dummies in a doll's house.

Because the writer is so interested in the world, they are hoping we'll see those bizarre restrictions and wring our hands for the poor characters. But that's difficult if we don't connect with them.

What's missing is life. The reader needs a sense of what those conditions mean.

Adding this life needn't be difficult. It can come from the most mundane details – going to work, shopping for food, getting an appliance repaired. Orwell's *Nineteen Eighty-Four* begins with an ordinary day in April with a few things off kilter, and builds into a skewed and frightening world.

I often advise dystopia writers to create the world, then test-drive it. Don't worry about scenes for the novel; explore for its own sake. Put a camera on a character's shoulder and follow them on an ordinary day. Let your imagination discover their peculiar difficulties so you can understand how they live. It might give you surprising ideas.

Also explore the regime. Unfair or repressive rules usually arise because the majority will conform. Perhaps economic conditions have forced it, as in Suzanne Collins's *The Hunger Games*. Or perhaps, like Ray Bradbury's *Fahrenheit 451*, it is because everyone helped create the society.

There will always be characters who are better adjusted to the world, and it's interesting to think about them. Ask what keeps them happy. Some people conform because they want a quiet life – even if they suspect wrong is being done. Conformists usually don't like to be reminded of this deal with the devil, and might feel very threatened by dissenters.

If there is a system of willing collusion, there will always be people who 'wake up', perhaps struggle with the strictures, maybe break free (like Guy Montag in *Fahrenheit 451*), or maybe get re-imprisoned (Winston Smith in *Nineteen Eighty-Four*).

If the society creates the regime, could you explore the way it evolved? The book-burning in *Fahrenheit 451* arose because of a mob rule that dumbed entertainment down. Why did they do this? Because they were at war. They wanted a comforter and tranquiliser, not a stimulant. And it suited the authorities to provide an anaesthetic that the population would take so willingly. In *Fahrenheit 451*, a state-of-the-art TV isn't a screen. It's a life-sized hologram in the living room. Soap opera characters and chat show hosts are known as the 'family' and the 'relatives', and viewers are more attached to them than they are to real-life friends, husbands and children. Books and especially literature are abhorred because they are private and complex; they reawaken awareness of difficult questions. And we see how brittle this utopia is, as these 'happy' people regularly attempt suicide.

The most powerful dystopias are plausible and recognisable. This works if we understand how they evolved and why people sustain them. Bradbury unpicks how his people created their own unstable, despairing society, and how it's consuming them. Moreover, we could find ourselves there too.

Dystopias come from characters.

Too many characters – problems with a huge cast

Sometimes a writer invents more characters than they can comfortably manage. They're often writing stories of big scope, about entire villages, countries or the crew and passengers of an ocean liner. So they create a plausible number of personnel, but can't think of enough things for them to do or ways to distinguish them. The result is a mush where one character blurs into another – and the reader can't remember who's who.

Of course, there is no upper limit on how many characters you can have in a story. It's the number you can cope with as a writer.

But don't assume that because your story world is big, you need a lot of major characters. You can still make it feel populated without a cast of thousands.

Your first goal is to keep the reader involved, and the best way to do that is by attaching us to individual characters in depth.

So how do you make your people more distinctive?

First, cull the unnecessary ones. Examine whether any duplicate the same dramatic function. Could some be spliced together, thus making one stronger character? Perhaps combining roles would create a character with interesting internal conflict. The friendly village policeman could also be the guy who sells black-market DVDs.

Some of your foreground characters may not need to be so prominent. Could they have lesser roles in the background, or even be human wallpaper like extras on a film set? More on minor characters later.

If a character has a very minor role, they may not need a name. When you name a character you make readers notice them. If there are too many who don't seem distinctive, that can be overwhelming.

Who do you need in the story? Your cast members should grow from your central characters. Identify the protagonists, then the people who are important to them – perhaps a boss, sidekick, best friend, partner in crime, family, arch-rival, inspirational teacher or mentor.

Also consider dramatic function. Some characters might stand for society, family, rebellion, authority, despair, hope. Not all of these will be major players. Some will be glimpsed rather than put in the spotlight.

Do you have too many main characters? Look at your protagonists and ask who they really need around them.

Send in the clowns – comic characters are jarringly obvious

Characters with humorous plotlines are very useful, especially to let air into a dark story. If your protagonists are going through unremitting hell, you can ease the tension with a lighter subplot and characters who are less troubled.

But it's easy to misuse comic relief. Some writers are too desperate to demonstrate the change of gear. The narrative style changes and is suddenly loaded with flip observations, as though we have stopped the action to watch a troupe of clowns. The narrative might even tell gags about the characters. It looks like a different novel. And if there is a scene where characters from the comedy corner meet those from the serious story, the writer is really in a twist.

The problem is the change in tone. Good novels make you feel like you've read a coherent whole, not several books pasted together. There's nothing wrong with gags if characters tell them. But it jars the reader if the narrative style starts to tell jokes where it didn't previously, or it becomes suddenly ironic or comic.

So how do you knit your comedy characters in?

Identify what makes these characters funny when others aren't. Is it their behaviour, attitudes, luck? Are they sweet and silly? Do they take life less seriously than their beleaguered friends?

Also, it helps to find something about them that isn't funny. You don't need too much, so no need to invent an entire family history or a buried tragedy if that will take the focus off your central characters. But give us just enough to see a rounded person.

The same applies for scenes where your most tortured characters have comic moments. Don't change the narrative voice. Let the comedy arise from what they do and say.

When writing comic moments, don't change your narrative voice. Let the humour arise from the characters' personalities, attitudes and behaviour.

Passive central characters

Some central characters do very little. The plot happens to them and they are pushed from one development to the next. The pressures on them mount, they get distressed – but do they do anything about it?

No, they wait for the next heap of merde to fall, then agonise some more.

These are passive characters and they tend to look feeble. Readers respond better to characters who are active, who cause things to happen. They might be unlucky or badly treated, but they aren't victims. Events make them fight back, which usually makes matters worse. Or maybe they invited trouble in the first place. The professor is flattered by the adoring attention of his pupil and encourages her, little realising she will become a vindictive stalker.

It's very easy for writers to make a character unintentionally passive. They create a situation, devise complications and add characters who will inflict the various misfortunes. They imagine it deeply and write interesting twists. But all the challenges come from others' actions.

Perhaps this indicates that many writers are passive. Maybe that's true; we are natural observers and analysers. And most of us would prefer trouble to fade away.

But we need a more active mindset when we write stories. Readers can get exasperated with characters who never try to take charge, solve the problem or counter-attack.

Sometimes the passivity is deliberate. One of my clients gave her character a quiet life because he had a past he needed to hide. He was always being upset by perceived threats, then wringing his hands and hoping nothing would come of them.

This became tedious, but it didn't take much to beef the character up. We thought of active measures he could take to hide his secret. This suggested consequences. With these small changes the character had me biting my nails and hoping he wouldn't give in to his urges... but I knew he would. A few more tweaks and the later events were slanted so that they were caused by these early actions – and the story started to take flight.

The passive central character can be a particular blind spot when writing in first person, because all the trouble revolves around them.

Stephenie Meyer's *Twilight* is commonly criticised for this. In the first novel, the narrator instigates nothing, she is simply kept on the run by the predatory chap who fancies her. In fact, she is a conduit for the reader to experience the events, and Meyer succeeds because the passionate writing and inventive plotting keep the reader gripped.

But with a different genre or a less enthralling story, that passivity could get irritating.

Although your central character might be unlucky or badly treated, don't leave them passive. Let them cause trouble too.

First-person narrator has no character of their own

First-person narrators can easily become a bland, characterless eye (or 'I'). The character has few distinct attitudes, relationships, history.

In some genres this is deliberate – the reader is intended to transplant themselves into the adventure (like *Twilight*). But if you're not writing that kind of story, don't forget to add the character of the narrator as well.

One of the most misleading discussions in creative writing circles is whether the reader will like our characters.

This term 'likability' is confusing. Many perfectly compelling novels feature a protagonist who is deeply flawed, badly behaved and a person to avoid in real life. Fiction lets us indulge our curiosity in complete safety. Main characters in novels don't necessarily have to be people we'd approve of, rely on, confide in or marry to our daughters.

Writers may also be confused by looking back on characters in novels they adored. They think of how they felt when they closed the book, not of how the characters seemed on first acquaintance. In many novels, the reader's feelings grow as they share the characters' journey. Attachment, admiration and affection may not happen instantly.

Indeed, our feelings towards the main character may become less positive through the book, rather than more. But that doesn't mean we'll stop reading. Done right, that can still make a satisfying journey. When great characters come to grief it's the stuff of tragedy, a glimpse of the temptations and forces we all might harbour in our souls.

Remember the discussion on switching viewpoint characters, and the writer who replaced a protagonist who went too far down a dark path? He could equally have stayed with this character to the appalling end. We had shared enough to understand the man's inner life. We had seen him overcome troubles and felt the pressures that might ruin this hard-won success. Although the writer might have needed to add a new character to receive our affection, he didn't have to cut the ties with his original one. The bond was there.

Although we don't have to like the character, we have to enjoy the time we spend with them. This connection is usually established in the first pages. Their personality might make them an interesting companion, like the disreputable and witty Humbert Humbert in *Lolita*.

We should also be curious. Their situation and mental state should hint that there is instability, disturbance; more to discover if we stick around. The character may have contradictions that promise to cause trouble: perhaps they're brave but also spiteful, or charming but thoughtless (you can find exercises to explore character contradictions in the section on character design: see page 161).

Relatability is important. It's good if we can see their humanity. Vulnerability is very appealing: if the character has a yearning need, a secret or a hole in their soul, that bonds the reader to them. You can even do this with the coldest fish. Patricia Highsmith's Tom Ripley is a cool, clever con man, but his first scene catches him at a moment of worry. He's being followed, and fears one of his schemes is catching up with him. The pursuer turns out to be an unexpected acquaintance; no threat at all. Ripley's confidence returns in all his calculating glory, but in those moments we see the past that might undo him at any moment.

Likability is one of the areas where novice writers worry too much and try too hard. If you're still struggling with this, I've listed common beginner pitfalls in a separate section (see page 177).

Characters don't have to be likable. Make us interested to spend time with them.

Recognition and the universal – keep asking 'why'

One of the most powerful ways to make readers bond with a character is to find a way they speak for us all.

Suppose you decide to write about a character who falls in love with a stranger she sees regularly at a railway station. She has a husband she doesn't want to cheat on, but nevertheless finds herself drawn to this other man (Noel Coward's *Brief Encounter*). This is a tangled problem that is bound to get worse – plenty to keep the audience intrigued. But what if you dug further?

For instance, how much was it chance? Could she have brought it on herself? Was she as happy as she looked or was she bored in her humdrum life and wishing for more excitement? Might many of us be her, feeling that our settled lives lack a certain thrill? We might all wish for romance, even though we are contented. The more you search, the more likely you are to find a universal hook. *Brief Encounter* could be seen as a story about a girl who felt life had become humdrum, as we all might. We recognise she walks a line we might all approach. And look what she unleashed.

Find your story's universal resonance. Keep asking 'why'.

🖋 If you show a scene that establishes a character's personality or traits, don't forget to include their reaction.

🖋 If a character has a dramatic need, make us understand why it is important to them.

🖋 Make sure the characters we are interested in have an internal life, even if you only show it in glimpses.

🖋 Create your enigmatic characters with intriguing details that tempt the reader to speculate on the truth.

🖋 If you feel unconfident writing a character because their background is very different from yours, examine what they want and what they fear.

🖋 If you're worried your characters aren't authentically masculine or feminine, use the Gender Genie. But don't forget authenticity also comes from historical and cultural details.

🖋 Give the characters a life beyond the central problem of the story.

🖋 Use background detail with care. Too little and the characters float in a void. Too much, and the story is suffocated. Show it in glimpses to create a complex and lifelike effect.

✍ You don't have to describe the character top to toe on first meeting. Use short, vivid impressions to convey their presence, and add to the reader's mental picture each time we meet them.

✍ If the character has to think about their appearance, find a good reason.

✍ Great misfit characters are not just different on the outside, in fact they may look average. Find out how they are peculiar in their soul.

✍ With teenage characters, create the person first and modify according to their stage of development.

✍ Consider the different faces your main character might present to the world.

✍ Although you as the author know a lot about your characters, give them the chance to speak for themselves. Show not tell.

✍ Once you've found what links your characters together, find what makes each of them distinct.

✍ If you change viewpoint characters late in the book, prepare the reader to welcome the new perspective.

✍ Choose a viewpoint character who will have an important reaction to the story or an interesting perspective – even if the biggest dramas don't happen to them.

✍ Make symbol characters work as people, and indicate their

extra significance with structure, language and imagery.

✐ Dystopias aren't about worlds. They're about characters.

✐ If you have problems making every major character distinctive, you might need to reduce your cast.

✐ When writing comic moments, don't change your narrative voice. Let the humour arise from the characters' personalities, attitudes and behaviour.

✐ Although your central character might be unlucky or badly treated, don't leave them passive. Let them cause trouble too.

✐ First-person narration doesn't automatically create a compelling character. Add attitudes, relationships, history to flesh them out.

✐ Characters don't have to be likable. Make us interested to spend time with them.

✐ Does your story have a universal resonance? Keep asking 'why'.

4 Change

Change makes a story worth telling. It gives the events consequences. It makes the story an important experience in your people's lives.

What should that change be? Anything you like. Perhaps the characters fulfil a dream, achieve a goal or catch a bad guy. In some genres that's enough.

Most of the time, a story will seem hollow unless the protagonist changes in personality or motivation (or both). And this change has to be dramatised in behaviour.

They might grow up a little, treat people better, solve a problem that held them back, reshape their priorities, break toxic habits or discover the people they belong with. Guy Montag in *Fahrenheit 451* becomes uncomfortable with his job and then his life. It becomes increasingly intolerable and pushes him to the fringes of society where he finds people like him.

Perhaps the characters don't change their lives. They might return to the original environment and not fit so comfortably. Conversely, they could grasp it with new elan. Maybe that has a sting. Frank Wheeler in Richard Yates's *Revolutionary Road* returns to humdrum suburbia, knowing that he's not nearly as daring as he thought. Fortunately the wife who embodied the urge to be ambitious is no longer with him.

Or perhaps realisation comes with a bitter taste. They get what they want, but regret they chose career over love.

Indeed, change doesn't have to be positive. Macbeth starts off as a hero, but as he succumbs to ambition he becomes increasingly ruthless until he is deposed. As long as we find the change interesting, it doesn't matter which direction it moves.

We must feel that this change is permanent. The events of the story must mark the characters, and for good. Readers love this. They get a primeval hit of satisfaction if they've witnessed a journey of private significance.

If this is missing, they're likely to shrug and think: 'so what?'.

Sometimes characters are looking for a settled place. Jane Eyre and Black Beauty travel through many 'families'. Both novels end when they have found where they belong. Their personalities don't change, although their motivations might. Jane begins by wanting to survive life with her brutal aunt. Then she must get through a bleak school. Then she wants to find a teaching position so she can be independent. Then she wants to marry Mr Rochester. Then she wants to escape and make a new life. Finally she wants to find Rochester again. She's essentially the same person, but her circumstances, priorities and conflicts change throughout the story.

Catalyst characters

Not all central characters have to change. There's an interesting breed whose personality or motivation doesn't change at all. They might be named in the story's title. James Bond, Sherlock Holmes and Doctor Who have personalities and jobs that cause massive upheaval. They blast in, sort out a problem and exit, exactly as they were when they arrived.

Many long-running series have catalyst characters, but they also appear in standalone stories. They may be intriguingly complex and unbalanced. Perhaps they are misfits. Other characters may try to reform or heal them, but with little success.

Catalyst characters don't have to be problem solvers.
An antagonist with the catalyst nature could be formidable. Mr Eccles in Patrick Hamilton's *Twenty-Thousand Streets Under The Sky* doesn't himself change, but he catalyses a change in the main character, Ella.

Catalysts might be mentor characters. These are figures who guide the protagonist into a new world, awakening the qualities they need to meet the challenges they must face. Typically they're a coach or a father figure. They sometimes perish when they have fulfilled their role, or in a betraying twist they might turn out to be a formidable antagonist, like Long John Silver in *Treasure Island*.

When the catalyst character departs, make sure they leave someone shaken and stirred.

Characters who resist change

What if your aim is to present a snapshot of a society where everyone does their best to maintain the status quo? Change is impossible – and that's the point. When writers tackle concepts like this, I encourage them to look more closely.

How are the characters keeping the peace? Is everything as stable as it appears? What struggles might they have? On the surface they might glide serenely, but under the water it might be chaos and conflict. (There's that power word: conflict. It's everywhere if you dig.)

Now, if all the characters are fighting secret battles, are they really not changed? Does it not take a toll? Do they not become increasingly desperate and entrenched? Could one character find it increasingly intolerable?

Many stories like this involve a society, but they just as easily might centre on a smaller, private situation. Imagine a couple trying to keep a marriage together, and the strain that might cause as it becomes more difficult. Indeed, it's common for heroes to initially resist change. Guy Montag in *Fahrenheit 451* would rather muddle along than accept his new feelings and act on them.

Readers need a whiff of disturbance to keep their attention. If the entire story is about characters resisting change, look for instabilities that will make the situation increasingly fraught.

For your toolbox

✎ Look for ways characters can experience an important transformation. It makes a story far more satisfying.

✎ Where characters try to resist change, find instabilities that will make the situation increasingly fraught and give the story momentum.

5 Villains and antagonists: what goes wrong with wrong 'uns

The terms 'villain' and 'antagonist' aren't interchangeable by any means, but they cause writers similar difficulties.

First, a definition. While a villain is necessarily an antagonist, an antagonist is not always a villain. They both cause your protagonist trouble − by opposing them, tormenting them or upsetting their lives. The period in which they clash will make your protagonist change.

But here's the difference. Villains intend real evil and destruction. They have perverse and ruthless tendencies.

Many of these are the features of personality disorders, although villains don't have to be clinically mad. To be villainous they might lack empathy; be driven by abnormal greed; want to destroy what others have; get their kicks from inducing fear and pain; enjoy manipulating others and preying on the vulnerable. They gravitate to situations where they can satisfy these urges.

Antagonists, on the other hand, are a wider group. They simply have an agenda that causes your hero trouble. They might be as humane as your protagonist, but simply have different goals. Antagonists don't necessarily have dubious morality or deviant personality traits, although they might.

The main problem with these 'enemy' characters is that writers don't develop them with the same perception and insight they devote to heroes. Or they are heavy-handed about signposting their enemy's story function. Perhaps this is because they're deeply involved with their protagonist or the causes they are dramatising. Maybe they can't imagine themselves into the enemy's world. So they build the story around the protagonist, and don't give as much depth to the other side.

That's a pity because foes can be nuanced without losing their menace. Indeed, they are fascinating characters because they can represent shadow sides of our own natures; the murky areas of hidden desires, moral struggles and unacceptable impulses.

Writers often focus only on the negative, but all antagonists have one strikingly positive characteristic – they are highly motivated and determined. If they weren't, they wouldn't cause such problems.

Here are the ways that antagonists go flat on the page and how we can bring them to life.

Writer puts the enemy character in solitary confinement

Many writers make their antagonists operate in isolation, outcasts from the rest of the story.

It's true that antagonists might be loners, but they don't have to be. They are just as likely to have supporters. They might even be more popular or powerful than your good guys, especially if they're at the villainous end of the spectrum.

Villains might have big organisations, which might or might not be evil. Whether this is a corrupt local council or a global company, it involves relationships. Who works for or supports the villain? Do they know the villain's true nature? Do they stay with the villain because of their own ambition, the salary, the villain's charisma or some other reason? Indeed, the villain might not be the boss, but a bright star tipped for success or an inconspicuous, hardworking junior in the postroom.

You might give your villain a key sidekick. A sidekick has an obvious use when the villain needs to explain their plans, but they can do more for you besides. You can use them to demonstrate what kind of person gets closely involved with the villain and how the villain behaves in relationships.

This can turn into an interesting dynamic. What keeps the sidekick loyal, especially if the villain is dangerous, possibly criminal and capable of real harm? Is the sidekick wary of the villain or brashly confident, imagining they will one day fill those shoes?

Perhaps the sidekick turns a blind eye because of duty, or is troubled but trapped, like the less bloodthirsty members of a Mafia family. Maybe the sidekick hopes to subtly 'save' the villain – in which they may or may not be mistaken.

Even if the villain operates alone, it looks odd if they never need an ally, even one who is shortlived. Perhaps they win the trust of others so they can get supplies or information. They might turn on unexpected charm, like Frederick Forsyth's assassin character in *The Day of The Jackal* who smoothes his way into a woman's bed so that he has a place to hide for the night. She doesn't live to see the morning. Patricia Highsmith's Tom Ripley is a character who doesn't need anybody on an emotional level, but nevertheless forms many alliances. These usually outlive their usefulness or become inconvenient. If your villain views other people as disposable, it's a shame not to show it in action.

Even when writers are tackling the less villainous antagonist, they tend to isolate them. So a divorcee who schemes to split her husband's new family will be depicted living miserably on her own, as though the story universe is already condemning her. It's more probable that she'll have support on her home turf. This might be the children from the marriage. Or a friend who doesn't like to see her unhappy. Perhaps she finds herself surrounded by other embittered divorcees who egg her on. Or perhaps nobody knows the plans she nurses in her heart.

Even if a character is so bitter they drive their allies away, it's more plausible if a new person reaches out to them. And it's not hard to find somebody who will, even with the most prickly antagonist. Priests or kind neighbours might extend a hand simply because most of us are social animals and don't like to think of a person on their own. This will help highlight the traits that fix the antagonist on her peculiar path.

If your antagonist is kept in isolation it will look unlikely and unbalanced. Give them allies and friends to round out their world and reveal the depths in their character.

Narrator intrudes to tell us who will turn nasty: foreshadowing the bad deeds

If characters have deviant and villainous natures, it can be good to prepare the reader before they act against the protagonist. Many writers will include a scene that introduces us to their skewed moral code. This is all good and necessary, but sometimes writers direct the reader too heavily.

One of the ways they do this is by shifting tone when those characters appear. So the villain-in-the-making will be described with extra adjectives and adverbs, like a neon sign flashing the word 'nasty'. If he sits back in his chair, he thrusts his chest forwards (pompously). If he walks past a beggar in the street, he gives a snort (disdainfully).

This bias especially comes across in dialogue. Where other characters speak or laugh, the bad guy will cackle. Even if the writer doesn't use the word 'cackle', their lines will have a gloating tone.

Of course, some authors have a lot of personality in their narrative style, especially if they write with a comic or satirical spark. But they will show this with all their characters.

It's similar to the problem of switching tone for comedy characters. The reader may not identify what's changed but they notice and might feel uncomfortably pushed to accept a particular view.

Cartoonish and cliched scenes are another way writers get heavy-handed when introducing antagonists.

As with the comedy characters, the writer needs to let the characters speak for themselves. Definitely make them sizzle with menace or thrum with menace, but use the same style as other scenes. Avoid the temptation to mock them or you might diminish their power. Keep the villain's world on the same scale as that of the good guys.

Charles Dickens is an interesting example. Although he might lampoon characters with colourful names and quirky tics, he is carefully plausible when alerting us to characters who will be trouble. In *Bleak House*, Harold Skimpole seems enchantingly childlike, but one of the first things he does is charm the generous Esther Summerson to pay off one of his debts. The law clerk Mr Guppy proposes to Esther, then stalks her creepily after she refuses him. When we see Guppy on his own, his obsession with her seems to have a scheming motive.

However much Dickens may adore adding colour, he doesn't use caricature when he warns the reader who will be a threat.

If you're creating characters who will ultimately cause harm, you can warn the reader in behaviour that is consistent with the rest of the action. Contrast a character who behaves kindly (like Esther) with one who abuses kindness (Mr Skimpole). Show what the character tries to get away with when he thinks no one can see him, and how he treats people in a weaker position.

Also, are you racing too far ahead? Sometimes the writer's awareness of the novel's climax will taint the early sections where the enemy may be simply selfish rather than villainous. This is hard to gauge, especially as we revise the manuscript multiple times.

It's also a risk if we have drawn from real life. Our feelings about our hero or our rotter can seep into the writing. If when we set up dastardly Derek, we're thinking 'he was so thoughtless and cruel', we may gallop ahead of the reader. However, if we adjust that to 'in this scene he seems appealing, if thoughtless', we can invite the reader on board.

When you establish characters who will turn bad, avoid the temptation to steer the reader with a loaded narrative tone or exaggeration. Give us glimpses of their negative traits in a way that's consistent with the story's world.

Bad to the bone – only negatives

Villainy is not for the weak and feckless. But many writers seem unwilling to consider what might be impressive about their villain. They often make them ridiculous too, as if telegraphing that no sane reader would approve of what they do. But villains often have strongly developed positive traits such as tenacity, ingenuity, intensity and energy. By necessity, they are original thinkers. They just happen to have channelled those energies into destructive goals.

Demonstrating your villain's strengths will make them a more deadly opponent. They become clever and unstoppable; a credible threat rather than a bad figure waiting to be brought down.

True villainy is fascinating as well as appalling. Fiction allows us to indulge our curiosity about people who behave as we would not. This starts with their talents – natural abilities and assets that are put to dreadful use. The unnamed assassin in *The Day Of The Jackal* is admirably resourceful. Thomas Harris's Hannibal Lecter is intelligent and cultured, and Harris's serial killer Francis Dolarhyde is vulnerable. Patrick Suskind's very singular serial killer Jean-Baptiste Grenouille in *Perfume* has an exquisitely well-tuned sense of smell.

In tragedy we often see strengths that turn destructive. A tragic hero is a great man with a fatal flaw, and they can be formidable villains. Shakespeare's villain Iago embarks on a campaign to destroy his general, Othello, by preying on Othello's jealous nature. Both men are jealous, in fact, but they are also proud, ambitious and determined — traits that served them well. Writers often create tyrants who lack any admirable qualities when instead they could enthral us with a great man or woman who overdeveloped a strength.

I also see this blind spot with antagonists who aren't evil but simply on the opposition. Just as writers are reluctant to let antagonists have friends, they often won't allow them any positive traits. As well as overdirecting the reader, this raises credibility questions. How can they pose a serious threat to the protagonist if they are inferior? And if the threat comes from their social position or job, how do they keep it if they have no employable or admirable qualities?

Make your antagonist more formidable, disturbing, credible and memorable by exploring their strengths.

Weak motivation for villainy

Villains might not be sane and they certainly don't abide by our norms of morality. But this doesn't mean we should leave their motives unexplored or vague. Readers are fascinated by the urges that drive a villain.

Often writers give their villains an abstract lust for 'power', which could mean anything and is hard to grasp. Like heroes, villains make more sense if they have recognisable goals. Perhaps they want to avenge a wrong or claim an inheritance they feel was wrongly given to someone else.

Their motives might not initially be negative. They could begin by struggling out of poverty, then find their ambition drives them like an engine. They might believe they can solve the world's problems. In fact, the lust for power is not by itself villainous. The villainy comes in the things they are prepared to do.

A plausible motivation makes the villain seem more determined. We know why their goals matter, and why they won't give up.

Villains go to places the rest of us don't dream of, so the more individual they are, the more impact they will have. Take the title character of Ian Fleming's *Goldfinger*. He collects gold obsessively and is pathologically greedy. He cheats at cards and golf even though his winnings are negligible compared to the wealth he already has. His plan to rob Fort Knox will kill thousands of people, but he can't see why this would worry anyone.

Many writers make villains do wrong for its own sake. Certainly there are personalities who get kicks from cruelty and destruction, and we'll discuss them in a moment.

But this is a small subset; most villains feel their behaviour is right. Perhaps they have a philosophy or religious conviction. Maybe they are in a criminal fraternity with its own code of justice and honour.

If they knowingly cause harm, perhaps they feel justified, like Iago. They might have flashes of conscience or doubt, or another character who reminds them of their good side, before their soul became so twisted. (This might put that character on a knife edge. Initially protected by the villain's affection, they might become an unbearable voice of conscience, which the villain may have to smother.)

Perhaps they do not notice the harm they do, like Goldfinger. To him, people are of no consequence; it's no big deal to cause death. On the other hand, they might be monsters of nightmare, relishing the hurt they cause.

Indeed, it's often hard for writers to make cruel characters nasty enough. We're peaceful, bookish, empathetic and constructive; we have to work hard to model characters who are none of those. We may have to break down barriers of our own.

Actors often say this; they might not like a villain, but they have to find why it's good to be them.

The key is in their motivation. Without victims, these characters get nowhere, so what rewards them? Perhaps, like Kevin in Lionel Shriver's *We Need To Talk About Kevin*, they feel powerful when they inflict physical and emotional pain.

And cruelty isn't a generic catch-all; it operates in individual and intricate ways. Maybe, like Heathcliff in *Wuthering Heights*, they feel they are righting wrongs that were done to them (which might apply to Kevin too, in a different way). Some people are just as satisfied to hurt strangers, feeling an animal rush when they cause fear, pain, rage or grief.

Whatever your villains do, if you delve into what drives them, you can make them more formidable, believable and memorable.

The nebulous enemy – the trouble with battling 'society'

In some stories, the protagonist is battling 'society', 'the system' or 'oppression'. But this can be too vague if it is kept as an abstract force. It works better if those forces are embodied in characters.

People are more threatening than organisations. They have instincts and intelligence that may root out our hero's secrets. In *Fahrenheit 451*, Guy Montag is growing uneasy with his job and his life. But the immediate threats don't come from a faceless society; they come from the people who act for it. His boss, Captain Beatty, represents authority. His wife and her friends stand for social norms. His colleagues are peer group pressure.

A cruel character can enrage us far more than an organisation or a regime. In Ken Kesey's *One Flew Over The Cuckoo's Nest*, the battles are fought with one character, Nurse Ratched. We loathe her for her inhuman tyranny, and thus we loathe the institution that put her in power.

Suzanne Collins came up with a smart solution in *The Hunger Games*. Her characters are forced into a gladiator-style combat where they hunt each other and win advantages for their town. Ideally they also have to outsmart the rotten system and salvage their humanity. The antagonist is society, but Collins turned it into more potent, immediate threats – the other contestants and the rules of the game.

Stories are about the particular. A distinct character; a distinct situation; a personal problem. The more you can personalise a conflict, the more a story will stir up the reader's emotions.

For your toolbox

✐ Give your antagonists allies and friends to develop their world and reveal the depths in their character.

✐ If you're signalling which characters will turn nasty, avoid the temptation to change narrative tone. Give us glimpses of their negative traits in a way that's consistent with your story's world.

✐ Give your antagonists good characteristics too. A fatal flaw is usually a strength misused.

✐ Don't skimp on your villain's motivation, no matter how extreme they are. If you delve into what drives them, you can make them more formidable, believable and memorable.

✐ If your characters are battling 'the system' or 'society', create antagonists who embody this.

6 It's all relationships: romances and significant others

Your characters live in a web of relationships. Family, comrades, rivals and bosses. People they're romantically involved with. People who make them feel good – or dumb. People they wish they could see more of. People they used to be tied to. People they're tired of. People they wish they were like.

Relationships can create a story world. In Donna Tartt's *The Secret History*, the narrator Richard Papen arrives at college to study classics. He meets a group of charismatic, fascinating people and because of this gets involved in a murder.

Everything in the novel happens because the people influence each other, and eventually have to break free.

My own novel, *My Memories of a Future Life*, was built from the characters' relationships. Everything the narrator, Carol, did came from what she felt about her significant others – her closeness to her friend Jerry; her unease about the hypnotist Gene Winter, who takes her to her future life; her curiosity about her next self, Andreq. She is a concert pianist, so her connection to music is a relationship too.

Relationships put characters under pressure or relieve it, just as plot events do. Again, in *My Memories of a Future Life*, readers were fascinated by the remote, manipulating Gene and his unnerving effect on Carol. Maybe if she hadn't come along, with her personality and problems, he wouldn't have been nearly so interesting.

In Daphne Du Maurier's *Rebecca*, the narrator is torn by her relationships. The husband she feels she's not good enough for. The servants who are the traditions of the house where she feels inadequate. The housekeeper Mrs Danvers, with her suffocating loyalty to Rebecca (a nebulous enemy made flesh, as discussed in the previous section).

Romances are incredibly useful in stories, even if hearts and flowers aren't your crowd's primary interest. There can't be a genre where love – particularly unrequited – isn't a handy motivation. If the relationship isn't the centre of the story, it can still drive a character's actions. But only if the reader believes in it.

So characters' significant relationships contain much fuel to power a story. Here's how it often gets misused or missed.

Rules of attraction: relationships that fail to grab the reader

A relationship can be the human heart of a story. Done right, the reader will bond with it and care if it is threatened. How do we achieve this?

Scriptwriters talk about the 'meet cute'. Often used in romantic comedies, this is a scene where future lovers show they are adorable when together. It only suits certain genres, but the principle is broader: the audience (reader) must believe your people belong to each other.

In conventional romance they might become sweeter or housetrained, but for other stories they might get violent, ultra-sexy, murderous. Perhaps they spark for other reasons. In Richard Yates's *Revolutionary Road*, April and Frank are attracted by a mutual ambitious streak. Perhaps the effect is unequal: one partner adores, the other abhors.

Quite often, writers ask us to believe that *x* falls for *y* but we never see how they affect each other. Without this, the attraction looks sham. A significant new partner gets into a character's marrow – they might feel challenged, calmed, completed, irritated, nervous, discontented, frustrated. (Or the writer might mention the change in passing but not show it – telling instead of showing.)

If the relationship is already established and we are asked to care about it, we must see why the characters fit together.

(The second point about the meet-cute principle? All storytelling is manipulation. If you dislike a trick because it is overdone by formulaic movies or novels, look for the string it pulls and find your own way to tweak it. Because pulling that string is important.)

Make the reader believe in the relationship and want it to develop.

Don't forget to show the moment it started

Quite often, two lead characters become a couple, but we don't witness it build or start.

For some genres that may be fine; relationships may not be important. But where they are, this blank spot looks peculiar, particularly if the novel shows other life events, friendships and allegiances.

Readers love seeing characters warm to each other, especially on such a private level. (Getting colder is interesting too.) Conversations become more honest and personal; characters let their guard down and laugh, or one cries on the other's shoulder. Maybe the closeness is sudden. One night they work late to sift case notes. Or detective A gets B out of a scrape and suddenly feels protective of her. This transformation builds tension and makes the reader more attached to the characters.

Of course, not all stories have room for spooning and courting. You can condense to just the scene where there's no going back. That needn't even be a kiss; it could be a word or a long look if the reader understands. But the do-or-die point is one where the characters take a chance and it's a pity not to show it in some form.

If you want the reader to invest in the relationship, show us the tipping moment.

Romantic dialogue and discomfort with moments of intense emotion

Sometimes a romantic scene draws us in, then the writer (unintentionally) pushes us away. We're with the characters, sharing every second:

> John glanced awkwardly at his feet, as if he needed a moment to find the right words. "What would you say if I told you...".

So what did he tell her? And what did she say? But we never find out because the writer rushes the rest with a few judgements:

> Fenella was overwhelmed, she felt very emotional towards John.

(That's another case of telling when it's better to show.)

Emotional scenes often give writers cold feet, as if they imagine all those readers judging their words. This is hardly surprising; in real life, we only have these conversations if we feel safe or brave.

But prose is private. Readers forget there's print in front of them. What they experience is as confidential as a dream. Good writers forget about spying eyeballs. They talk to the page. In this type of scene, the more honestly you share, the more real the characters will be – to readers and to you.

Of course, it's possible to over-splurge; I'll deal with that later. But if you never venture into your characters' vulnerable moments you'll keep the reader at a distance.

It takes practice to get comfortable in these scenes, but it's also rewarding. Often you can surprise yourself when you let characters reach out to each other, then keep writing to see what they do. This isn't to say that you can't have a discreet fade when a scene starts to boil. But know why you are withdrawing. It may be a deliberate style choice, a genre convention, considerations of the reader's age. But don't pull away because you don't know how to show it. Try sticking with the scene a little longer. Forget about the readers and talk to the page.

Leaning on strong words instead of engaging with the characters

This is another way that writers shy away from characters' emotions. They wield handy words like 'love' and 'upset' and hope to convey great turmoil:

I felt hurt by her curt remark and I became very upset. I began to fear she didn't love me any more.

Not very convincing, is it?

Most of us don't write about strong emotions until we get noveling. Nothing else we do prepares us for it. Even if our day jobs involve describing how people feel − psychiatrists, counsellors, journalists − it's likely to be detached and analytical. In those environments, words like 'hurt' and 'upset' are hot keys that carry an impact. But they also allow the reader to keep a professional distance. In novels, though, we don't usually want distance. We want the reader involved.

Before we drown in generalisations, a quick word about distance. Sometimes it's just what we need. The character might be referring to an episode way in the past, or being ironic, or inviting the reader to dismiss it (which they may not agree with). Most of the time, though, the writer wants us to feel the sting. So we need to see this curt remark and understand what was bad about it. (Show not tell.)

There is another reason why this line has a false ring, particularly the second half:

I began to fear she didn't love me any more.

Unless the character is displaying deliberate detachment, this isn't how people talk about deep worries. They often don't admit what they really fear, even to themselves. If a remark gets under their skin, they might find excuses:

'she's been under a lot of pressure', 'sometimes she doesn't know what she's saying'. 'She always says that but she doesn't mean it'.

If I read that, I believe the character is worried.

Sometimes, stretches of a manuscript sound like the author making notes, instead of the characters living the situation. You, the writer, may know that Jim fears his wife no longer cares about him. But there's an extra step to making it real for the reader. Instead of 'hot-words' and summary ('hurt by her curt remark'), we need to create those feelings with action and dialogue. And instead of letting Jim draw a shocking conclusion instantly, we should explore how he wants to deny it's true.

More about dialogue later (see page 128).

Where characters splurge their feelings

We shouldn't feel the writer is holding back. But we love it when characters do, particularly in scenes that involve deep feelings. You can stir up a huge charge from what is left unsaid – and indeed may be unsayable.

When you drafted your manuscript, you might have opened the floodgates. Those are your private workings. You're limbering up to explore what your people really say. But sometimes authors leave too much in, writing pages of unfettered gush. Certainly you want the characters to sing their hearts, but you don't want to rob them of dignity.

Here's a challenge. If a character confesses their attachment, try not to let them say: 'I love you'. Instead, make the reader hear it.

The phrase isn't forbidden, but many writers use it as a magic wand, hoping it will add instant drama and intensity. In fact, what the characters mean is more important than the actual words.

What can they say instead? Anything that fits with the normal business of your plot, but make the reader understand 'he's telling her he loves her'. If you've built the tension, this is where you can trust the reader to fill blanks.

Perhaps one character tells a story that's more personal than usual, but could be dismissed as 'just a story'. The other might respond in kind. Or might not notice. Or might ignore the hint. Whichever way it goes, it sustains the tension. The reader completes the equation with their own reaction. Which is very satisfying.

Of course, there are situations where a blurted 'I love you' is perfect – maybe as a shocking outburst from a character who is overwhelmed or backed into a corner. Or you could deploy it to devastating last-ditch effect, like the moment Princess Leia has to leave Han Solo in *The Empire Strikes Back*.

If the characters do confess so unmistakably, they must react. That may seem obvious, but often a writer rattles off a quick, startling 'I love you' and both parties carry on as before. Even if they're outwardly cool, the temperature must change. They could become more comfortable together – or the opposite.

Let the characters act with restraint if that feels natural
to them.

Startling confessions erupt out of nowhere

Sometimes a character declares a violent passion to another,
apparently with no warning. This can be powerful, especially if
other characters also find it shocking. But it can easily seem
random and inconsistent. Why?

Because when it works, it's not sudden at all. The writer has
usually been laying subtle clues. They'll plant them in the
character's personality, minor reactions and behaviour. As
readers, we may not notice them. They might serve another story
purpose, meanwhile making a path of hidden stepping-stones to
that moment. The reader, wrongfooted, will think the scene's
power comes from the violence of the surprise. But because of
this preparation, they'll also accept it.

Almost any sudden story development needs to be seeded. If
your characters are in the mountains and there's going to be an
avalanche, we must, without being obvious, introduce the idea
that avalanches happen. It's not enough that the laws of physics
make it possible. That's too random for stories. The same applies
for emotional avalanches.

And don't forget the consequences once the snow has settled.
How do the other characters react? Also, the character himself
must acknowledge he's passed a point of no return.

If you give the impression that the character's emotions erupt at random, that can look implausible. Use stealth to prepare the reader to accept the development.

Sexual tension for bashful writers

Some authors write sexual attraction as confidently as any other kind of tension. Others are unsure how to broach what their characters are feeling, and become hilariously discreet.

In one novel I critiqued, the writer had a scene where the male protagonist bumped into a female colleague at the gym. She was wearing a swimsuit and her hair was wet. They talked earnestly about work – a good detail as they were trying to act normal. But here was the problem: the author gave no hint that this was a struggle. As I read, I forgot one of them was wearing wet Lycra and the other was disconcerted. They might as well have met, fully pinstriped, by the photocopier.

The writer told me she hoped the situation would speak for itself. But there are limits to what the reader will add. And when something surprising happens, we need the writer to guide us.

Quite understandably, this author was hoping she didn't have to spell it out. But you don't have to describe palpitations. Instead, suggest the disorientation of seeing a colleague in a swimsuit, the surprise of softly toned arms and smudged, sleepy-looking eyeliner.

And if the point of view allows, what does the woman think? Is she flattered, wishing she'd brought a bigger towel, or hoping her goggles haven't left red marks around her eyes?

Although sexual tension is a potent force, in most stories outside the erotica genre it's rarely just about sex. It's another way for characters to influence each other, control or be vulnerable (or both). It adds a charge or complications to a plot situation. Indeed, if it doesn't, it shouldn't be in the book.

If you find sexual tension awkward to write, concentrate on the story function.

Too coy about seductions

Seduction scenes really test our boundaries. Everyone has a different comfort level for what they can happily write – and read. For most genres, you can be as discreet as you like. Except for certain specifics.

It's all about the story. The seduction of an important character is an advance in a relationship. It breaks boundaries, creates commitments or consequences. It requires trust or represents a betrayal or abuse (or both). This is what you must not leave out.

But writers do. They're so worried about getting their characters together that they leave a big gap. One moment we're privy to the characters' interior worlds, following every moment, feeling the tension build. Next time we see the characters, they're arm in arm as a matter of routine. This can make the reader wonder if they just missed 20 pages.

When you've been showing a story moment by moment, it looks very uneven to race past a significant development. You can fade to black at the purposeful raised eyebrow, the front door, the secluded alleyway. But don't leave out the moment when the relationship entered this new phase.

Lexicon of love: how to describe sex

How closely must you describe what characters do? First, establish what is expected of your genre. If you're writing erotica, readers put their money down for details, just as thriller fans expect excitement and violence. Also, examine what you need the scene to achieve in the story. Perhaps you have a rough gangster and want to show his tender side; in that case, write the scene to emphasise atmosphere and affection.

In most novels, intimate details aren't remotely as important as the scene's plot function. There is always something else going on that develops the overall story.

If you're going to mention anatomy, what words should you use? Each genre has its own vocabulary. Erotica will have a range of slang, fun names and four-letter words. In other genres you can use euphemisms, metaphors and similes, as appropriate to your taste and level of courage.

Don't duck behind cliches. Some writers do, even if they carefully avoid them otherwise. Their secondhand nature will jolt readers out of your story and it makes you look embarrassed.

I had one writer who did a great job of making us want her characters to clinch. At bedding time, she tried to sneak a cliche past with this cheeky phrase –

Kirsty couldn't help but respond with the Mills and Boon staple 'I want you now!'

Please: no.

Sometimes you can describe the physicality with absolutely no x-rated detail. In Jane Smiley's *A Thousand Acres*, the protagonist has a fling with a handsome neighbour. The narrative draws a veil at the actual assignation, but this encounter has the fallout of a nuclear bomb and afterwards she dwells on it endlessly. She tortures herself with futures that seem impossible and others that seem intolerable. Of course it would look odd if she didn't think about the actual sex. She does – vividly, obsessively and with extraordinary discretion:

'what he did and what I did, and what he then did and what I did after that, seductive, dreamy, mostly wordless, renewing itself ceaselessly'.

If you're going to follow your characters to bed, find a descriptive level that suits the tone of the novel and the atmosphere of the scene. And however much fun they're having (or otherwise), don't forget to keep the scene advancing the story.

Special friendships need glue

So far I've concentrated on romance and sex, but if your characters have special friendships, we need to believe in them also. For instance, why does the withdrawn, shy kid like his best friend? Because he gives him confidence and makes life fun?

Perhaps it's not all positive. In Michael Frayn's *Spies*, the narrator, Stephen, is looking back on an intense childhood friendship with Keith. Although they met because they were neighbours, that's not the only reason they hang out. Stephen finds Keith exciting. He likes Keith's house and family, because they are less embarrassing and humdrum than his own. Stephen shelters under Keith's dominant personality and lets Keith instigate their games. We don't get Keith's perspective as it's first person, but Frayn hints that the arrangement appeals to him for various reasons too.

Close friendships can do a multitude for a story. Even if they are not the central trajectory, they can show a softer side to a character, give them something to worry about or fight for, create conflict. For that to work, we have to believe they have strong roots and can't be discarded easily. Find the special glue that binds your characters together.

Special friendships must come to life

If a main character has special people they often confide in, we need to see their relationship in action. But some writers will hide their scenes and give us only a swift summary:

Sitting in the coffee shop, Ashley told him about the events of the day.

or

It was on her mind so she talked about it.

If the friendship isn't significant, a summary like this is fine because it treats the friend as an accessory; like a coat or handbag that can be brought out as needed. (More about this in the section on secondary characters.) But if the friend will help the protagonist through the events of the plot, they must come to life in their own right. The relationship might well change – deepen, go cold, become more trusting. It might snap under the strain.

If your main characters have people they rely on, show us the friendship in action. (Show not tell.)

Relationships have their own landscape and language

A good way to bring a relationship alive is to give it special places. Indeed, a relationship can look curiously untethered from the story world if it doesn't have landmarks.

For a romantic couple, what is their favourite restaurant, the place he proposed? If their affair is illicit or forbidden, is there a haven where they can be alone? Is it tricky to get to? Are there people who help make this possible?

Families have extensive territories. The childhood home and neighbourhood, the place they often went on holiday, the grandparents' houses. Where Dad or Mum worked – which might be so far away it's no more than a significant name. If the family moved, the next home might always be 'the new house', even if they spent 10 years there. These places embody the power of the past. They do not feel like anywhere else.

It's worth taking time to think about these territories. Even, take your characters there as an exercise and notice how they react. You might not use the scenes in the book, but it's very unusual to find a character who doesn't have special places that are connected with important people.

People who are close also develop their own language, arising from shared experiences – particularly catchphrases. These might come from films they saw together, TV, or the memorable antics of friends: wearing a wrongly buttoned shirt might be called 'doing a Sarah'. These phrases embody a history that bonds the characters to each other and reminds readers of their history.

Find the places and words your characters associate with their families, lovers and friends.

Happy families

Many writers brilliantly show the joys and truths of being a parent. When the kids are small, they drag the characters into daft, absorbing games. They use Mum's Yves St Laurent lipsticks as crayons. They blurt out the rude secret names Dad invented for tedious family friends. And of course they can unlock Mum's mobile phone.

At the more grown-up end of the scale (and before the era of lipstick and gadgets), writers have other ways to show parents in thrall. Elizabeth Bennet in Jane Austen's *Pride and Prejudice* is her father's favourite, because she alone shares his inclination for ironic banter.

But some writers get stuck on intense, unconditional devotion. They create parents who are soppy, sentimental and cloying; stereotypes, not individuals. They write how the poor mite feels safe in the father's strong arms, and the mother is protective as a lion. Both parent and child frequently think (or worse, vocalise) how much they love each other, without a trace of humour or irony.

In fantasy particularly, children are apt to think about how wise their parent is, again in complete earnestness.

This only seems to happen when writers show well adjusted families. Troubled, abnormal homes are described in startling and believable detail. Supportive ones, though, are often bland, identikit or syrupy.

But even if the character's home life is not in the centre of the action, it still needs to ring true.

In *Wolf Hall*, Hilary Mantel is mainly concerned with Thomas Cromwell's life at court. His family ticks along in the background, typical and average, but it's still distinct. He is charmed by his children but also worried and baffled. One of his daughters loves Latin and Greek. In Tudor England, what good will that do her? He wishes he could graft her gifts into his son, who's a fine lad but academically slow. Mantel creates a warm heart for the book, but one that feels rough and real.

When you show a happy family life, don't create stereotypes. Include the worries and trials as much as the wonders.

Relationships that end their journey too soon

Some novels are the story of a relationship. But I see a lot of manuscripts where it peaks too early.

We see the relationship start. The writer builds it carefully, makes it plausible and perhaps destined. Half-way through, our guys hook up and we feel a sense of hard-earned achievement. Phew, they're friends. Or dance partners. Or lovers. Or reconciled. The end is still a long way off so we wonder: what next?

But the narrative plateaus. Another hundred or so pages unfold, and nothing much changes. These fortunate chaps continue on the same harmonious note, right until the end.

When this happens I suspect the author has created the story as a long fantasy of perfection. That's entirely their own business. And we all get involved with our creations. Letting go is hard, especially when we spend so long making the reader root for them. If we do write many scenes of indulgent bliss, we should keep them to ourselves because they look very flat in the finished novel.

There are two solutions. One is to rejig the story so that the characters don't reach harmony until the end. The second is to add new problems, such as outside events that put them under pressure or in danger. Or keep the relationship in flux. Maybe it warps with the wear and tear of life. Perhaps one character dominates, then the other. They might want different things, or change their expectations. They might develop no-go areas that are never admitted to. Maybe it disintegrates. Perhaps they relearn how destined they are, and seem to have earned it all the more.

If a relationship is one of the story arcs, whether it's a family tie, a friendship, a romance or a working partnership, don't plateau too soon. Take the arc all the way to the end.

For your toolbox

🖉 If the reader must care whether a romantic couple are driven apart, make us root for their relationship first.

🖉 Readers love to see the special bond forming.

🖉 Don't dodge emotional scenes – the reader notices the gap. If you're inhibited about writing them, forget about the readers and talk to the page in private.

🖉 If your character confronts a shocking truth, explore how they might express their fears in an indirect way.

🖉 You as a writer can't hold back. But your characters can.

🖉 When a character erupts with a long-suppressed emotion, make sure you have laid subtle clues.

🖉 Seductions and sexual tension are essentially scenes about control, trust and vulnerability.

🖉 If you're going to follow your characters to bed, find a descriptive level that suits the tone of the novel and the atmosphere of the scene. And however much fun they're having (or otherwise), don't forget to keep the scene advancing the story.

✒ If your characters have special friendships, show what glues them together.

✒ Find the locations and phrases your characters associate with their families, lovers and friends.

✒ When you show a happy family life, don't forget to include the trials as much as the wonders.

✒ If a relationship is central to the story, design it with an arc of its own.

7 Supporting characters and walk-ons

Supporting characters and walk-ons help to flesh out your novel's world.

Some of them have significant roles: a buddy for your protagonist to hang out with; a shoulder to cry on; a wise mentor; a sidekick who is less troubled than the hero; a therapist who helps (or hinders). Their job is to reinforce, encourage, perhaps add humour or some other perspective. They might also bring out your protagonist's strengths and add complications.

Some secondary characters might be confined to certain environments and locations: the local shop; the school gates. They will have more extensive lives, of course, but these are not relevant to the book.

Some peripheral characters are little more than plot devices on legs. They bring an important parcel, repair (or condemn) the car, get in the way when your hero is rushing down a street, dither in the shop so your hero can't close on time. They're usually seen only once or twice. These people mustn't steal too much attention, but they have to feel real. Here's where they go wrong.

What secondary characters talk about

What should secondary characters talk about? Anything that you or I would: what they like; how their holiday went; TV shows they follow; mutual friends they saw recently.

But some secondary characters are extremely limited in their conversation topics. They talk only to fill us in on the plot or main characters.

In some stories this is plausible − perhaps they are part of a police investigation or court case. In Graham Greene's *The End of the Affair*, the central character engages some private detectives who remark on the plot events and comment on the wider themes of the novel. It's plausible for them to do this, given their personalities and roles in the story. Otherwise it can look odd (see the section on dialogue for a discussion of exposition). In stage drama you might create a chorus of secondary characters who comment on the action, but drama has a symbolic quality where this can be readily accepted. It is often too artificial for novels.

Secondary characters should certainly illuminate the novel's themes. But this must come from their lives and concerns. You need to hint that they also operate independently of the book. Give tiny doses of the following: aims, goals, agendas, worries, people they adore, rivalries, obligations, ambitions, troubles, passions and scores to settle.

It can be hard to make this up on the spot, so it's worth deciding one or two details in advance. Solidly realised novels are backed by a lot of preparation material that never gets used on the pages. It remains at your fingertips, to use in tiny glimpses that make this character different from that.

Secondary characters who don't have lives can look like a ghostlike chorus of puppets, but when a writer has done this imaginative work, the novel is more convincing.

Work out what your main secondary characters do when the central folks aren't around.

Secondary characters need less screen time: use summary

Although secondary characters must be tangible presences, they don't need the spotlight. Summary is a useful way to keep them in the story without stealing attention from your principal players. For instance, if you want to show they meet your narrator regularly:

I went to the Tate Gallery with Janice. Her sister's shop went bust so she's now temping in the office up the road. We walked around looking at Mondrians and talking about people we remembered from the writing course.

Note that you can't write a paragraph like this if you don't know how your secondary characters are connected with your main folk. But just a few details are enough to convince.

Of course, the narrator might talk to Janice about events we've already seen. In that case, you can summarise those and cut straight to Janice's reaction:

I told Janice all about it as we stood gazing at the simple primary-colour blocks of Mondrian. She said, with equal simplicity, that Peter was lying.

Or cut the preambles and start the scene late:

'He said he had nothing to do with it.'

Janice shook her head. 'If you ask me, Peter's lying.'

One of my clients was having trouble handling his heroine's friends. He wanted them to regularly see each other, but didn't want to write scenes of inconsequential chat. So he found story reasons to prevent them meeting. Every time his heroine had a lunch date, it would be cancelled. If she phoned to catch up, it would be a bad time to talk. After a few of these episodes, it looked as though everyone was avoiding her. But when he showed these scenes in summary, he could write the encounters without repeating material or giving them undue emphasis.

And could you give these encounters more purpose? As discussed earlier, scenes are more satisfying if they have more than one function. While the characters are catching up, could you also advance the plot or illuminate a facet of the protagonist or their situation?

If you're writing encounters with secondary characters, it's fine to summarise, and to enact only the material that is important to the main characters or moves the story on.

Supporting or peripheral characters must contribute to the story

Supporting characters need to do more than eat lunches, drink sympathetic tea and answer the phone. Their presence in the book must be justified. Sometimes it can look as though the writer has spliced them in solely to have a change from the main action.

Not all characters have to directly affect the plot. Perhaps some of your supporting players have a textural role. They may stand for normality, or the central character's problem taken to its worst outcome. They may present an alternative take on the story's theme. Maybe they flesh out the lives of characters who are not the main focus of the story. But characters with these functions still have an effect in the book.

Every character, no matter how unimportant, should add something – even if only textural or thematic.

Walk-on characters in too much detail

Some novels describe all the cast members in fine detail. Even the insignificant chap from the gas board has tics, a name, a detailed physical description and sometimes even back story. This can be a tad overwhelming, because readers feel obliged to remember these details.

Maybe the writer believes this makes the world seem real. Actually it doesn't, because it's not how perception works (more on that in a moment). Or perhaps their outline contains all this detail. Or maybe they changed their mind about how important a character would be.

Good writers learn what to leave out. The detail may well exist, but you don't need to show it all. And if you downgrade a character, don't forget to trim the amount of attention you give them.

How do you strike the right balance? Try thinking about your own life. Most of us encounter walk-ons every day – the postman, the pedestrian who thanks us as we brake for them to cross. We notice perhaps one thing about them, if that, but they are still real.

So the postman might have a wedding ring, home-cut hair, a right-sided limp and egg on his shirt, but we'll only notice if we have reason to. If not, he delivers the letter and is gone.

Walk-ons are wallpaper. They are props to make the world of your principle characters believable; teeming ants to populate a place or a life routine. They are not there to grab the spotlight.

They don't need a name unless there's a reason – perhaps the postman's name tag reminds a bereaved character of someone she's lost. But notice how this detail serves the atmosphere or the main character's mental state. It's not about the postman. He isn't a life, he's a role.

Sometimes, though, a passing stranger is more than that: for instance, they witnessed a murder. You want the reader to notice but not to twig they're important until later.

So hide them in plain sight. Give them an action that looks like background colour. Perhaps they ask your protagonist for parking change. Or they cause trouble because they can't get their dog (or griffin or butler) under control. You can make this look insignificant while the protagonist has their mind on something important. It's even better if the event mirrors the mood of the scene or something in the protagonist's mind, such as a feeling of disorientation or frustration – then it keeps the focus on your main character's experience. Later he can suddenly remember – wasn't there a guy with a dog (or griffin or butler)?

What about Charles Dickens? He's a stand-out rebuke for this rule. He revels in his walk-ons, describing them all in fantastic, funny detail, no matter how minor. Well, for one thing, he published as he wrote, so didn't always know how significant a character would be. Most of all, though, he was rather good at it. And if you entertain that trumps everything.

Find the minimum you can do to let us know the characters were there, but don't burden us with irrelevant material.

For your toolbox

✎ Figure out one or two things that your main secondary characters do when away from the central folks. It's much easier to sketch this out beforehand than invent on the spot.

✎ Use summary in scenes involving secondary characters, so that you keep the emphasis on the main character's story.

✎ Every character should add something – even if only textural or thematic.

✎ Walk-on characters don't have to be given a full physical description, a name or a history.

✎ If you need a walk-on to be significant later, hide them in plain sight.

8 Dialogue: more than a transcript of speech

Characters come to life through dialogue. It's one of the most involving ways for a reader to experience a story.

Real-time conversations are one of the main ways we show instead of tell, which by now you should agree is a Good Thing Indeed.

Dialogue also makes a book easier to read, but not just because the paragraphs are short. Dialogue is immediate, of the moment. It has an energy that draws the reader onwards.

Many of the issues I've discussed have involved dialogue. Now let's look at it in detail.

No dialogue

Some writers turn in manuscripts that are solid narrative and hardly any dialogue. Unless you're aiming for interior monologue or stream of consciousness, this can look muted, like seeing the characters through a filter.

(Indeed the purpose of interior monologue and stream of consciousness is this constricted viewpoint – as though we are eavesdropping on a character's thoughts and observations.)

But what about first-person novels? The narrator is in charge of everything the reader sees. Can they get away without dialogue?

That depends on your intentions. First-person narrators usually leave room for other characters to be themselves. Although the story is all their point of view, they still let other characters behave independently. Indeed the novel will seem dull if other characters don't surprise them or spoil their plans. Those twists work best as encounters in real time – dialogue scenes.

Sometimes first-person narrators are intended to be unreliable. Dialogue lets you hint that your storyteller might not speak the whole truth, or doesn't have all the facts, or is more innocent or embittered than some of the other characters.

So dialogue is pretty indispensable. But many writers leave it out when they shouldn't. Why is this?

First of all, writing dialogue requires a mental gear shift. You stop being the author in charge of the narration. You have to give your mind to your characters, feel their concerns and the ways they speak and behave. It's like being a movie director who is also playing one of the parts. One moment they're omniscient; then they walk in front of the camera and forget that to join in the story. It's just as tricky to change back.

Secondly, a novel written with little dialogue may flow beautifully – to both reader and writer. I can't count the times I've written a passage I'm pleased with, then realised I'll have to butcher it to let the characters speak. But without dialogue, characters can look like dumb players.

If you've written your novel without much dialogue, was that a style choice or because the narrative ran away with you?

Flow is the crucial principle here. Try returning to the scene on a different day to add the dialogue.

Beyond talking

Sometimes we get so focused on making characters talk that we forget to let them perform non-verbally.

Speech is only one part of dialogue. Characters might pause, think, gulp in surprise, gasp with laughter (although probably not all in one scene). Writers often don't realise they can use silence, especially for shock. They try to write the words the character would say, but it sounds false because many people don't verbalise in this situation. Often, they are robbed of their words.

If it fits the character, let silence be their reply. If they've been highly amused, don't make them say how funny something was; let them laugh. Pauses and reactions can be just as eloquent as speech, and they effortlessly demonstrate when a remark has had an impact.

Don't forget you can use non-talking responses.

Remember we see dialogue as well as hear it

By nature, dialogue scenes are aurally vivid; they give us what an eavesdropper would hear. But prose has to feed our other senses too, especially visual.

Your words aren't just a microphone, they are a camera. We need to see what the characters do, otherwise the reader can feel blindfolded.

Some writers have to make a separate pass to engage their visual sense. That's fine. Dialogue probably takes more drafts than any other kind of scene — as you'll see later when I discuss the layers you can add with inequality and subtext.

Visual description also makes dialogue read more smoothly. A page of 'he said ... she said' can be monotonous, especially coming after descriptive passages.

Some writers' styles change in a jarring way when they write a dialogue scene, but if we include character actions and visuals we can ease the transition, allowing the narrator to stay present.

Don't forget the visual elements in a dialogue scene.

Internal reactions too vague

In an earlier section, I discussed characters who seem to have no internal life. Internal life has to continue in dialogue too.

A good conversation – in real life and in stories – provokes reactions. Even more so in a novel, where every scene must change something. So characters must be affected by the things they're told, and we need to see this – unless you're aiming for a sparse style, or can rely on the reader to add reactions.

Characters also need to react to what's between the lines, depending on their personality (I'll talk about that in a while).

Sometimes characters show immediately what they feel. That's easy to write. But maybe they keep their reaction for later, remaining outwardly controlled. Or they seem to accept everything because they need to think it through. In a subsequent scene they will ruminate, romanticise, bowdlerise or fulminate.

These delayed responses are all tricky for the writer because they're not happening at the time.

The mistake is to show us the calm surface and not hint that more is brewing. Make sure we know, before the scene starts, what the characters really think and feel. Then we'll be able to guess when another character's words make them seethe or panic inside.

Of course, this depends where we are in the story. Once we know what matters to the character, we will understand when they are practising masterful control or struggling with something too big to articulate. In those scenes, the writer's restraint encourages us to share the tension. You might still show small betrayals of stress – a pause, a fidget, a bitten lip, a tight sound in the throat. These actions might increase the feeling of strain.

It also helps if we understand why the character won't show what they feel. Are they too good mannered? Do they want to deny the other person the satisfaction of seeing them upset? Do they need to avoid crossing them, for instance to keep their job? If they're generally inhibited, make us understand this is their usual mode.

But we mustn't mistake this calm control for a lack of reaction.

When your main characters are talking, keep us in touch with their internal life.

If a character keeps their reactions hidden, make sure the reader understands this.

Characters talk about distressing things without getting upset

If I asked you to think about a troubling event or problem, your heart rate would rise and you probably wouldn't think so clearly. Your voice might wobble; you might get aggressive or defensive. However much you hid this, something would show.

Novels being what they are, characters often have to share upsetting experiences. Unless they have already adjusted to them, it looks very odd if their emotional state doesn't change, even if they're trying to keep control. Sometimes, writers leave this out, which creates a strange, detached impression.

When your characters verbalise their distress, make it affect them too.

Author interrupts too much and slows the pace

Although there's a lot more to dialogue than talk, be careful how much extra material you add. We don't need to nurse the reader through each beat of the characters' reactions or what they're physically doing. The reader may not have to know that the character rotated the salt cellar in his left hand while he spoke.

Dialogue scenes usually read fast. The short paragraphs, the sense of the characters breathing and speaking, make it run swiftly in the reader's mind. When you interrupt for stage directions, internal musing or context you risk breaking this momentum.

In the early chapters you need to add more detail, especially about the characters' concerns, but later the reader will be tuned in. As the novel soars to its climax, you want to increase the pace. Too much interruption might dilute a gripping scene. Again, this is hard to judge for yourself, and you might need feedback from critique partners and beta readers. Once we know the characters, we will feel their triumphs and disappointments without having so much explained. Set them up so that you don't need to add as much context in later scenes.

Eavesdrop on real-life dialogue and there's a lot going on. Maybe neither person is listening to the other and they are having separate conversations. Or they are paying attention, but one person is leading. This person gets to change the subject. One of them might hardly acknowledge what the other person says, while their companion responds to everything.

This inequality might be because of a professional relationship. Perhaps a shop owner wants to keep their customer happy or an employee has to defer to a boss. Families are rife with hierarchies. But dominance and submissiveness is also evident in conversations between friends, who you might assume were equal. Even if they're discussing something neutral such as where to meet, someone gets the final veto.

Dominance dynamics are innate and fascinating. They're particularly obvious if you can erase the words. In my gym there is a bank of TVs, all showing different channels which you tune to with headphones. But it's a lot more interesting to watch them without the sound.

One day, I saw two boxers at a pre-fight press conference. The little guy was clearly in charge. When they stood in fight stance for a picture, he decided the pose; the other boxer obliged like an amiable bear. When the photographers finished, Little Guy was first to break away, giving Bear a comradely pat on the shoulder. Their different natures were so clear. Little Guy felt entitled to take charge and Bear was letting him. I'm not a boxing fan, but I almost wanted to see how this would play in the ring. Perhaps

Little Guy would win on ferocity. Or Bear would let Little Guy wear himself out then floor him with a good slug.

Of course, boxers are more aggressive than average, but this dynamic came from their personalities and chemistry, not their occupation. In non-physical situations you might have the boss deferring to the more self-assured employee.

Dominance is a fundamental of social interaction, and not just for humans. Horses, for instance, are highly socialised and some racehorses can be so intimidated by another horse's personality that they won't dare overtake, no matter how hard the jockey rides.

Back with homo sapiens, dominance will also arise from the social situation. Think of bewildered parents being controlled by their four-year-old's headmistress – or indeed their child.

Dominance becomes clear when you subtract the talking from conversations. If you watch dialogue scenes or interviews with the sound off, or people across a room, you might see how their personalities rub together.

Good dialogue in stories reflects the characters' true relationship and some of that will come from status and personality. When you throw a couple of characters together to make a decision, they need not be equally influential. Even identical twins have a leader-follower relationship. Identify who is calling the shots.

Do you need to complicate so much? Not always. Depending on your purposes, you may want bosses in charge and parents firmly in control. Your scenes may have enough drama and change. Your genre may not have room for such levels. (But you may be able to have fun with subplot characters, reversing the dynamic in a teacher-pupil or master-servant role.)

You might be surprised where a tweak might take you. Friendships might not be totally equal. Perhaps one character is irritated by the other, or amused by them. Is one more demanding? More needy? Does one think the other is prettier, richer or luckier? Is one gritting their teeth while the other is happy as a clam? Are the characters in competition on some level?

Are they attracted to each other? Is one in thrall and the other not? Is one showing off? Resentful? Do they feel circumstances have forced them together? Jane Austen revels in characters who endure the company of people they would rather avoid, or have complicated reactions to. Her dialogue sizzles with pent-up complications.

Most conversations in real life are unequal in some way, however subtle that inequality is. Even if the participants don't have an agenda, they will usually have subtle and interesting imbalances.

In fiction, you can use those differences to add depth to your characters and spice up their relationships. You might even use them to generate tensions and complications in the plot. What might this unevenness lead to?

It's even more interesting if this status fluctuates during a scene.

Imagine a husband and wife taking a car trip. If they argue about reading the map, the husband might feel he has the superior status. If the wife changes the subject so they are talking about arrangements for their daughter's eighteenth birthday party, she seizes the territory and feels in charge. Some blatant stereotyping here, but a change in control can be applied to any situation and make a powerful scene.

They might not even be having the same kind of conversation. One character could be talking about how to fix a rusty plough. The other character might take offence because he doesn't think he should be told what to do.

Good dialogue isn't just about the content of the characters' conversation. Look for the inequalities that reveal the nature and subtleties of their relationship.

What else might be happening under the words? Subtext

Conversations in fiction can keep a lot unsaid. Characters might talk about a simple plot aim, but really mean something they can't say overtly. It might be their attraction to one another (as discussed in the section on relationships), or a resentment they can't bring into the open. Readers love to spot what's between the lines, especially when they know the characters well.

They also love when a dialogue scene shifts something in the characters' relationship. It might bond the characters more closely together. They might become aware of this, but stick to the apparent subject of the conversation, not wanting to break the moment. Or they might be pretending to agree, but moving their allegiances elsewhere.

And that's not the only use of subtext. Just as the characters might have a hidden agenda, the novelist might too.

'You shouldn't have had it grilled. The meunière's better.'

says the slimy diplomat Sir Bernard Pellegrin to Justin Quayle in John le Carre's *The Constant Gardener*.

This is dialogue with several storeys of subtext. First, the characters: Pellegrin is referring to Quayle's unwise choices in other areas than dining. But the author is also playing with layers because this expresses the novel's theme: of people veiling their meaning behind diplomatic language. And it tells us the kind of posh, smug creep that Pellegrin is. We have subtext, theme and character all in one line.

On the other hand, we have to be careful. It's important not to get so obsessed with 'clever' dialogue that we cram each line with overtones and undertones. Often, word choices are meant to be noticed subliminally rather than studied for their glorious secrets. Sometimes a cigar is just a cigar, and people really do just say, 'Have a smoke, old chap'. There is still plenty going on in this simple line (relationship, scene-setting).

Subtext can also be useful if your novel might be read by a mix of younger and older readers. Romantic developments, sexual politics or sophisticated rivalries can be smuggled in for the readers who want it.

Readers love to spot what's unsaid in dialogue, especially when they know the characters well.

Long speeches instead of conversations

Some writers give their characters very long speeches, but these can look artificial. A screed of monologue is disorientating and we can forget there are other souls hearing it.

It's particularly odd if one character lists everything they want to say, then another answers at equal length. (Although it's easy to write the scene that way.)

Of course, you may have a good reason why everyone else is silent. Perhaps it's a wedding and the best man is giving his speech. Or a character is making a difficult and impassioned revelation, and commands absolute attention.

Less stressfully, a character might be briefing a team. Or they might be at a debate where one side makes a case and the other then replies.

Although the listeners might not talk, don't let them disappear from the room. Give them some silent reactions – grimaces, foot shufflings, lip-bitings, chuckling. Don't forget noises and visual details from the setting. Perhaps sounds of traffic or birdsong, or waiters tiptoeing up to take an order. But if you embark on a long speech and forget to ground us in the environment, the reader often feels that the scene has drifted off its moorings and is somehow not right.

Unless there is a reason for the other characters to keep quiet, it is very unlikely that they will. If your gang boss is briefing his minions, let them ask questions, make remarks or other exclamations.

Dialogue usually works better if most of the paragraphs are short. Conversations are generally more believable than speeches.

But sometimes a character has earned the right to a monologue. If so, don't forget to keep us in the scene.

Be informal

Sometimes writers are too formal in dialogue. Speech is looser than written prose, and conversations don't have to proceed in complete sentences like an essay. Allow some sentences to trail off. Let the characters talk in fragments or begin an utterance with a conjunction or even a curse.

'She's gone, has she?'

'Went yesterday. House is too quiet.'

'Only I thought you'd need someone to walk the dog.'

The casual tone sounds natural and conversational. There's give and take, a sense of one person responding to the other. This disappears if we fill it out:

'I hear that Julia has left. Is that true?'

'She went yesterday. I'm finding that the house is too quiet.'

'I ask because I realise that you might need someone to walk the dog.'

Although this version would satisfy your English teacher and your Word grammar bot, it lacks life. There are too many syllables between the important words — including several 'thats'. It flattens the characters' individual voices.

Indeed, in the first version, the fragmented sentences create an interesting mood. Are the two characters close? They seem to be sharing the same train of thought. Perhaps they naturally understand each other, which might bring them closer as the story goes on. Or is one of them sad and unable to talk about Julia's departure?

In this context, the shorthand sentences give the scene a feeling of reserve, with greater depths below. But when the sentences are filled out to be grammatically correct they lack this authenticity.

Although some characters might always speak in formal sentences, don't make it a default. Use fragments to make dialogue more lifelike.

Dialogue used as information-dump: exposition

Obviously characters have to explain stuff to each other from time to time. This is known as exposition.

Exposition isn't always bad. Indeed, a novel with no exposition might be incomprehensible. But often it's mishandled and the number one way is in scenes where characters explain something they don't need to talk about. Who are they addressing? The reader.

So character A explains laboriously about the oil production history of Tennessee to someone who already knows about it, doesn't have to know, and doesn't need to indulge the speaker. He listens only because it's important that the reader gets it.

Sometimes, the writer hopes humour will let them off the hook. So our expositing character makes a forced joke about the oil production history of Tennessee. Maybe the other does too, in a horrid phoney double act.

Another variation is where the writer shares the exposition among several characters. Character A says one chunk. Character B takes up the story. Add it up and you have the reader nicely lectured on the oil production history of Tennessee. But if the reader hadn't been spying on their lives, they wouldn't have said any of it. What's more, they often don't even sound like separate individuals – it's clear the writer took an essay and cut it into separate lines.

There's also the 'as you know' scene, where characters talk about their own histories for no reason:

> *'As you know, when we arrived on this planet three weeks ago and found there was no one at the base...'*

So how do you give the reader background information? Simple: find a reason why the characters discuss it. Or write it in the narration, just as you might handle back story or description. But don't contrive a scene where the characters explain it to each other.

Generally, info-dumps in dialogue are best avoided – but you can make them work if the other characters need to hear them.

Desperately avoiding the info-dump

Dear me, you're damned this way too. For every writer who forces characters to explain the obvious, I see a writer who valiantly tries to avoid it – but leaves the reader confused. So the characters talk about only the latest developments but the reader is floundering, unable to grasp the bigger picture. Unless your aim is this disorientating effect, it's not a good idea.

Find or create a character who needs to be briefed. Then you can pull the reader aboard and sail on.

Characters talk about events we have already seen

Of course, characters must talk about the events of the novel. They might gossip, update a friend, let off steam. But some scenes are written only to document that characters chatted about an event we've already seen.

Readers expect that each scene will show something new. If you revisit an event, you should give it a fresh purpose. Perhaps you can show it from a new perspective. Or use the conversation to create a bond, a rift or other interesting frisson. The characters might have different agendas, which polarise during the conversation. Their status might change, making them feel differently about each other. One might talk about how she is going to marry a sailor, not knowing the other character is secretly in love with her.

But if all you intend to show is that two characters kept each other updated, you don't need to show it in detail. A summary will do.

Try to find something new for the scene to do – show us the friend's reaction, the increase of tension or the change in relationships.

Most of the plot presented in dialogue

Dialogue can reveal plot developments to the reader. This is good if the reader wants to see the characters' reaction, especially if that's more interesting than the event. In first-person narratives it might be your only option anyway.

Some plots, however, are entirely reported in dialogue. Obviously this isn't wrong as many stories are told as witness accounts, but some writers do it because they can't change gear from 'talk' scenes. If there isn't a story or style reason, presenting all events as dialogue can look strangely limited, and destroys the sense of a real world where characters breathe and act.

If most of your revelations come through characters' conversations, try changing some into action scenes.

Thinking out loud, in quotes

'I need to do more thinking and less talking,' she thought.

Although it's technically correct to put quote marks around a characters thoughts, it creates the impression that they are uttering them out loud. Dropping the inverted commas is perfectly acceptable (unless you intend the character to talk to themselves as a deliberate tic).

'Who is that?' she thought

becomes

Who is that? she thought.

Or you could write the thought as part of a stream of internal musing – sometimes known as free indirect. This is better because people don't think in complete sentences. Free indirect is a more faithful reproduction of the way the brain works:

Who was that? He looked familiar.

(And you don't need to use italics either. I've done so only as a style device in this book to differentiate quotations and examples. Typeset the thoughts as though they were part of the main narrative.) Sometimes characters think with stage directions. They go through a pantomime of nodding, sighing or smiling to themselves.

Was that why she said those hurtful words? It had to be. William nodded to himself.

Although nodding and other physical responses are important when characters are in conversation, they look hammy if characters do it when alone. And it doesn't help the reader understand the situation better; that comes from context. Unless there is an extraordinary reason, characters don't need to mime their thoughts or say them out loud.

Too many social niceties and nothing interesting

Sometimes, writers stuff their scenes with trivial dialogue. Encounters with postmen, neighbours, waiters, flight attendants and others are narrated in their entirety.

'Good morning.'

'How are you?'

'I'm fine, how are you?'

'I have a parcel for Mrs Twistle.'

'Oh I'll take it for you.'

'Lovely hyacinths she's got.'

'Aren't they? I can't grow them myself.'

'That's my wife's favourite colour.'

'My mother likes that colour too.'

'I'll put a card in her door about the parcel. Much obliged.'

'It's no trouble. Good morning.'

As I read this, I'm waiting for a punchline. Or a vital clue. I'm wondering why my attention is being drawn to the parcel, the hyacinths or Mrs Twistle's absence. Perhaps the person who answered the door is being held captive by a gunman, and so the apparent normality adds tension. Will she let the postman know she's in trouble? Or maybe the scene is intending us to savour its normality, perhaps as relief after a bizarre and destabilising adventure?

But no, the writer intends no extra significance. Neither are they shooting for a post-modern reflection on the artificiality of novels, the details we forget every day or the pointlessness of existence.

That's an awful lot of lines to spend on ... nothing.

Although it would be strange if characters never said anything inconsequential, we need to strike a balance. It's fine to abbreviate the unimportant parts of a conversation. A few lines go a long way:

'Your Chablis, sir.'

or

'Do sit down.'

This same problem arises when major characters have downtime. For instance, they meet for a casual day out. Because they are major characters the writer records every sentence. Was the train ride all right, is the fish good, where shall we have coffee, isn't the weather awful. Let's go into the cheese shop, and nod as the owner recommends the Brie. We'll nod some more when he tells us where to buy wine. Oh and we must mention TV, and characters no one else has heard of. Crikey, will anything happen that's worth talking about?

As always, writers need to examine what the reader should take away. Is it closer knowledge of the people and their relationship? Is it a change? Did the characters develop a bond? Pointless chat won't show this, so delve deeper. Use subtext to explore the boundaries being pushed and adjusted. Look for walls being erected, status being challenged and changed. Maybe your scene is not as edgy as that and the characters are simply enjoying their day. Lose the dull details and bring out the enjoyment.

As I mentioned earlier, scenes like this can build narrative tension. Ruth Rendell's *The Keys To The Street* has a sequence where a couple have an ordinary evening. They order a takeaway, chat, pour wine, remark on passers-by in the street. It looks like bliss, but because of its position in the story, we fear it will be shortlived.

A little trivia is authentic, of course. But it goes a long way. Use inconsequential dialogue sparingly – and to bring out the real purpose of a scene.

What vocabulary does your character use?

We don't all sound the same. Literary professors don't speak like dairy farmers. Politicians don't talk like nurses. Our language is shaped by our lives, present and past. But some writers give characters a vocabulary that doesn't make sense.

This is especially noticeable with writers whose voice has a quirk — and let's face it, we all have characteristic words we favour. They create our personality on the page, which is no bad thing. But when all characters speak and think in that key, regardless of education level or personal style, it can look odd.

This especially shows with synonyms. Writers whose style is formal might choose 'witnessed' instead of 'saw', 'begin' instead of 'start', but will all their dudes do that? Similarly, if your voice is casual and slangy, will every character refer to vehicles as 'wheels' and being short of money as 'skint'?

Personal style will also show in sentence constructions. University-educated characters might think in elegant sub-clauses. Streetwise bruisers might have one plain idea per sentence.

Of course, a novel is its own special world. Your quirks might enrich the speech of the people you invent. It might make glorious sense if characters use unexpected language. Gangsters might posture in iambic pentameter. Infants might sound inscrutably academic and schoolteachers might mumble in monosyllables. Fairies might be filthy-mouthed. But these effects are the result of a conscious style choice.

It becomes a problem where the writer isn't aware how their natural style puts unlikely words into the characters' mouths. And especially if every character has the same tics as the narrator.

Word choice in dialogue is part of characterisation. If you're aiming for a natural style, match your characters' speech with their personality and life.

Going yokel

So here's the flipside of the above. The dialogue that's over-colloquial, ungrammatical, accented or full of funny pronunciations.

> *'I mean, I wouldn't believe any of it neither. Mu'ila'ed. That's it. And lying thurr the way she was. Wiv dem fings.'*

Dialogue like this is a labour to read. Odd spellings and dropped syllables make the reader stop to puzzle out the word, which throws them out of the story.

Of course, some novelists use this to interesting effect, like Russell Hoban in *Riddley Walker*:

> *We ben the Puter Leat we had the woal worl in our mynd and we had worls beyont this in our mynd we programmit pas the sarvering gallack seas.*

Riddley Walker is set after a nuclear holocaust, two and a half thousand years in the future. Society is primitive and the book is narrated in an evolved English of phoneticised spellings and fractured words. 'Gallack seas' are galaxies, 'Puter Leat' are computer elite.

The reader gropes for familiarity, which puts us into the mind of the narrator as he tries to understand the ruins of civilisation. (It also warns of our own fragility if something so fundamental as language is not permanent, but I digress.)

In *Riddley Walker* this is a poetic effect, but phonetic and mutilated language slows the reader. It can be comic, of course, and more so if other characters also struggle to understand. But it's just as likely the reader will skip, especially if the rest of the prose is conventional and easy.

If you need to draw attention to a character's distinctive speech and you want us to read it, tics are best kept to a minimum. You can remind us of it indirectly:

He heard the Scots burr in her voice.

And don't forget the effect of vocabulary, word choice and sentence rhythms. With all those devices, you hardly need phonetics.

As always, though, if you've got it, flaunt it. Accent with abandon if you can do it as well as Bill Bryson in *Notes From a Small Island*:

'Hae ya nae hook ma dooky?' he said.

'I'm sorry?' I replied.

'He'll nay be doon a mooning.' He hoiked his head in the direction of a back room.

'Oh, ah,' I said and nodded sagely, as if that explained it.

I noticed that they were both still looking at me.

'D'ye hae a hoo and a poo?' said the first man to me.

'I'm sorry?' I said.

'D'ye hae a hoo and a poo?' he repeated. It appeared that he was a trifle intoxicated.

If you need to draw attention to a character's distinctive speech, less is more. Use just a few tics, if at all.

Characters all sound the same – funny voices part 2

So each character needs their own voice. But writers latch onto the wrong thing: the word 'voice'.

I had a manuscript where a writer attempted to differentiate his characters by giving each of them an accent or vocal tic. It was like that weary joke with the Englishman, the Irishman and the Scotsman. When he ran out of regional lilts he added a cockney lovable who gorblimeyed in rhyming slang, a solemn Russian who made every word sound like 'borscht' and an upper class ass who couldn't say Rs.

I was reminded of Dickens's character Sloppy in *Our Mutual Friend*, who reads the newspaper out loud, 'doing the police in different voices'. At school, my Eng Lit teacher found this very jolly, but I wanted to stuff him into his own mangle.

Dickens, of course, ran a literary variety act. But there is more to his characters than funny voices. Render the dialogue in normal words, and you see vanities and pretensions, or heartbreaking stoicism. You see the person's individual attitudes and what they think of their fellow men.

Going back to my client's manuscript, when I stripped out the ochs and lisps, the characters all sounded the same.

Odd mannerisms, costumes or tastes are part of characterisation, but the core of it comes from within.

Also, we need to choose conversations – and conversation partners – that show how our characters differ. This comes across in their hopes and fears, ambitions and motivations, attitudes to risk and the moral code that guides the way they treat others.

Although vocabulary and vocal tics help you differentiate characters, identify what they would reveal about themselves if you wrote it all in the same style.

All characters have the same sense of humour

This is another way characters become homogenised. A writer often grafts their own sense of humour onto their characters, not realising their quips and quirks are all similar. Humour style is very individual and it can be a great way to differentiate characters.

There are many distinct humour personalities. Imagine a group of friends relaxing, and think of the different ways they could lighten the mood. Some might torture everyone with puns and wordplay. Some might make self-deprecating comments. Others might make remarks that paint their friends as rabble-rousing hell-raisers. Some are surreal and whimsical. Some, indeed, might smile with the others but never volunteer a humorous observation. We can probably add further variations from other cultures.

Humour styles might betray deeper attitudes. One character might always be pessimistic. One might always be trying to keep everyone's attention.

What about characters who tell clichéd jokes? There's a danger that the reader will assume the writer is being lazy, so it's generally a good idea to make another character groan or tick them off.

Identify your characters' humour styles and you have a clue to how they think and a further layer for their distinctive voice.

Bossy dialogue tags

Sometimes writers try to direct our feelings about a character by using strong dialogue tags.

The simplest dialogue tags are 'he said' 'she said'. They're plain and hardly noticeable – and that's the problem. Most of the time we're striving to make our verbs active and interesting. Also the repetition bothers us: 'said' turns up a lot in a dialogue scene. So we can end up with a stream of dialogue that runs 'he snorted', 'she shouted', 'he averred'.

First things first. 'Said' is practically invisible. Where possible we should find other ways to let the reader know who just spoke, but 'said' is so common that the reader doesn't mind seeing it repeated. These stronger synonyms, however, are conspicuous and can give your narrative voice an intrusive quality:

> *'We need to search the ambassador's residence,' announced Sarah.*

> *'I can't have your people running amok in the house,' pontificated Mr Tummelwicket.*

> *Sarah took a moment. How was she going to convince him? 'If we don't do it tonight, the Swedish maid will have left,' she pressed.*

> *'The last time your people blundered into there you smashed a Ming vase,' wailed Mr Tummelwicket.*

I feel like the writer is in the room with the characters, pointing to them and yelling: 'do you see? That nice Sarah's trying to do her job and prevent more murders. That twit Tummelwicket is obstructing her. And his voice is silly.'

Although 'pontificate' and 'wailed' are delicious words, they intrude. This is fine for satirical or comic effect, where the narrator might be a presence, but too heavy if your narrative is transparent and neutral. The more the reader is involved in the scene, focusing on the characters, the less they welcome the writer intruding – which is what these speech tags do.

That's not to say you can never stray from 'said'. For moments of unusual emphasis, it can be very powerful to write 'she whispered' or 'he called'. But they work only if you've kept your other dialogue tags unobtrusive.

A variation of this is the adverb. The writer will embellish 'said' with 'loudly', 'emphatically', 'winsomely', 'loftily', 'blushingly', 'angrily'. Scriptwriters call them 'wrylies', where the writer tries to use directions to indicate a speaker's tone or attitude, instead of conveying it through the action and dialogue.

Used sparingly, the adverb has power, but many writers are tempted to overuse. Keep for special occasions.

As an exercise, draft the scene without tags. Write what the characters say, add physical action, pauses, responses and other non-verbal signs of life:

> *She fiddled with her car keys, looking into the grain of the table as though the answer was there. Finally she took a breath. 'I don't know what we should do.'*

Then add just enough 'saids' to make it clear who's speaking.

Don't worry about repeating 'said'. Use a synonym or an adverb only if you need special emphasis.

For your toolbox

✎ If your novel has little dialogue, was that a style choice or because you got stuck in the flow of narrative?

✎ If you find it hard to shift out of your 'narrator' voice, try writing your scene's dialogue on a different day.

✎ Ground your dialogue by including non-talking responses.

✎ Don't forget the visual elements in a dialogue scene.

✎ If a character keeps their reactions hidden, make sure we understand they are seething under the surface.

✎ When characters verbalise their distress, make them act it too.

✎ Good dialogue isn't just about the characters' spoken lines. Look for the push-pull under the surface.

✎ Readers love to spot what's unsaid, especially when they know the characters well.

✎ Conversations are generally more believable than monologues. But sometimes a character has earned the right to a speech.

✎ Although some characters might speak in formal sentences, beware of making it a default. Use fragments to make dialogue more lifelike.

✎ Generally, info-dumps in dialogue are best avoided – but you can make them work if the other characters need to listen.

✎ If characters talk about the events of the novel, make sure the scene also shows us something new.

- Characters don't usually need to mime their thoughts or say them out loud.

- If most of your story revelations are reported in characters' conversations, consider rewriting as action scenes.

- Use inconsequential dialogue sparingly – and to bring out the real purpose of a scene.

- Word choice in dialogue is part of characterisation. If you're aiming for a natural style, match your characters' speech with their personality and life.

- If you need to draw attention to a character's distinctive speech, less is more. Use just a few tics, and sparingly.

- Characterisation in dialogue comes from within, from the hopes and fears in the characters' hearts, from different views and motivations.

- Identify your characters' humour styles and you have a clue to how they think and a further tool to create their distinctive voice.

- If your characters swear, give them different curse personalities.

- For most of the time, write 'he said'. Keep synonyms and adverbs for moments of special emphasis.

9 Character design: questionnaires and other games

A while ago I came across a website that sold bespoke romance novels as a gift for couples. The customer was invited to choose a setting from a list and answer some questions to personalise the story. The loved-up pair would be sent a story 'all about them' – a ready-made plot where their names, car, holiday preferences and favourite food had been pasted in. And eye colour – very important for scenes of dreamy gazing.

It was clear that none of the answers would be allowed to mess up the prewritten story or suggest interesting tangents. And superficial questionnaires can be pointless as exercises for novelists. Although you might need to decide your characters' eye and hair colour and so on, it's much more productive to spend time on exercises that enrich and challenge your story ideas and help you assert your characters' individuality. You want answers that create consequences. If possible, you also want them to forge connections with other characters.

Here are some character-development games I like. Adjust details and depth of exploration for your genre as appropriate.

Be a creative vandal – a warm-up

This is a warm-up rather than serious development. Imagine you are the most awkward customer possible for a novel whose characters will slot into a template. Take their questionnaire and try to break it.

What car does your MC drive? Make it a camper van with a leaky roof and grass growing inside. No scene inside that vehicle will be bland, and neither will the bohemian soul who owns it.

What music do they listen to while driving? They don't use music as background because they want to listen to it properly. Or the guy daren't play music while driving because it's too distracting, whereas the gal can't settle without her friendly tunes. Or she's an opera singer trying to learn a piece, and plays the same aria over and over, driving the guy potty. Or he and she can never agree on what to play.

What are the names of their best friends? His best friend is a rugby player called Tom. Hers is her cat, which he is allergic to.

What do they dislike? Her: flying. Him: salsa dancing, painted fingernails and hairstyles that remind him of his ex. (Try fitting that into a template plot.)

Where did they meet the love of their life? Him: Jamaica, a year ago. Her: in the salsa class she went to last week, on her own... (Now the template plot is in tatters.)

These answers may be partly facetious but they suggest consequences, motivation, conflict and connections. It shows how the answer to a question about a character needn't be a superficial box-tick.

Now here's a more serious warm-up.

Make your main characters different from you – but still write with insight

It's easy to create characters that are carbon copies of ourselves. Even if we invent a different life history, we might give them our own attitudes, approach to life, goals, responses to stress, desires and betes noires.

Many writers spend a lot of time on plotting and research – the stuff the characters will be doing. They don't spend time thinking about how their main characters tick as distinct people on a deep level – and how they might be separate from the writer who is inventing them.

Why does that matter? Because we may write one character with depth while the rest are stereotypes. Or we may repeat the same main character, novel after novel. We become like an actor who plays the same type and never develops a range.

But our most sincerely realised characters come from our deep emotional knowledge. We have to understand what it's like to live as them. If there's only one of us, how do we do that?

In fact, we all have many characters we could create. They come from the contradictions in our nature, the sides of our personality that we show or hide at different times – especially when we're under such stress that we don't recognise ourselves. And we all have certain friends or family members we understand so well that we could model what they'd think and do. All of those could be used to understand and write a wide range of people.

This exercise is not about what happens in your novel. It is about you. We're going to find all the characters you could inhabit well enough to write.

1 Reread The Double Life of Isobel (see page 54). Consider the many people you routinely are in your own life – the diligent employee, the protective parent, the confident creative, the doubtful dreamer, the frustrated perfectionist. Write them all down.

2 Now we'll look at what's inside them Don't see these as moods or superficial roles. They are personas who have different behaviour and feelings. You inhabit them naturally and with conviction. They convince you and the people around you. How do you do it? From shifts in confidence, self-esteem, social ease, worries and priorities. Especially priorities.

One of the fundamentals of a fictional character is what they want (and don't want). Take your list of characters and isolate a few details that distinguish them – what they desire, how comfortable they feel, how tolerant they are. Also think about what they might be afraid of – for instance, in some personas you might be more anxious about social acceptance. Each of these differences can be used as the kernels of new people.

3 Think about the ways your life could have gone Your choices got you where you are right now, but what if you'd taken that other job, married that other person? Can you draw out other personas from that?

4 Think about the people you have special chemistry with, who change the way you feel and behave Write down the people they make you into – and a few words to capture their qualities. Don't just focus on the positive. Include people who trigger your bad and ugly sides. (No one need know it's you.)

5 Many of us find we're transformed by music or by reading other fiction If there's a musical piece or a story that empowers or disarms you, revisit it and see if there's another character you can tap. On one of my blogs (mymemoriesofafuturelife.com) I have a series called The Undercover Soundtrack, where writers discuss using music in their creative process. Many of them find signature pieces for their characters, to help them inhabit their mindset and feelings.

6 Dig even deeper Go back to the section just before Izzy – A Carnival of Odd Misfits (see page 47). Find the parts of yourself that are never exposed to others, the impulses and worries that only you know about. Maybe you experienced them in very rare and temporary moments, but they can still be part of your repertoire.

Write down who those people are, what they want and what they fear.

7 Don't forget friends, family – or even rivals and enemies We all have people we'd know well enough to write (although see the discussion earlier about the need to adjust them).

You should now have a list of distinct defining characteristics, which you can isolate or blend to build truthful characters with motivations you understand.

Make your main characters different from each other

Now you have a range of characters you can connect to personally, it's time to use them in your novel. These questions are designed to alert you to fundamentals of personality and past, how your people click (or clash) with others, and how the story will challenge them.

First, identify what roles you need to fill. Then answer these questions. Do not answer as yourself – use personas from the list you identified in the previous section.

Not all the questions will be useful for all characters. The list is huge. Ignore whatever seems irrelevant, but delve deeply if you feel something stir.

1 How do they appear to others? Are there general traits everyone would agree on – brave, bullying, cowardly, talented, confident, mean, vain, shy, enthusiastic, needy, dreamy, artistic, unadventurous, serious, intolerant, pragmatic, practical?

2 What first impressions does the character create? When other characters know them better, do these change?

3 How does the character see themselves? How does it compare with 1?

4 Do they wish they were younger, older, taller, happier, more tragic, better educated? Do they try to project a false image of themselves? Was there a period they regard as their golden years or heyday?

5 What is their occupation or life role? Do they feel they are a good fit for it? How much of their identity is tied up in this?

6 What is their greatest pleasure? What is guaranteed to cheer them up?

7 What is their greatest extravagance? Why is it extravagant?

8 What are they good at and how does It matter to them?

9 What they are not good at – and does it bother them?

10 Have they ever been in love? Has their heart been broken? Do they still need to get over this?

11 What are their dreams? Do they tell others about them? Do they make decisions based on those dreams or do they feel that is unrealistic or impossible?

12 Do they daydream a lot? Do they live in memories?

13 Do they read? What are they reading at the moment? Memoirs, true events or fiction? If they read fiction, what kind – young adult, English classics, thrillers, fantasy? Do they prefer newspapers to books?

14 In their life right now, who are they most annoyed by? Is there a reason? Might this seem irrational, petty or perverse to others?

15 What are their biggest worries and stresses? Are they aware of all of them? Are there any they can't admit to? How much do these affect what they do in the story?

16 What is their greatest fear? Is there anyone they would confess it to? Who would they never tell? Is there something they fear but can't or won't discuss?

17 Do they have a secret? Is there anyone who knows it?

18 Do they hold any grudges? Is there something they cannot forgive another character for? Or is life too short to waste on grudges?

19 Who is their closest friend and confidante? Is this the person they would like to be closest to?

20 How do they treat others?

21 Who are their other friends and family? Are they close to them, distant, estranged? Which family members do they admire or despise?

22 Where does the character live now? Have they always lived there? If not, what do they think about their original home and the people they lived among?

23 Does the character have any nicknames, past or present? Versions of their name they now no longer use?

24 What strong memories have stuck with them from childhood?

25 From their past, who they would like to meet again? Who they would avoid?

26 Are they well travelled or have they always stayed at home? Which places are important to them, and associated with significant people?

27 Are they political? Religious? Have they always been, or did this start in a particular life phase?

28 What's their dominant facial expression – smiling, dour, tired?

29 What do they regret?

30 Do they have any treasured objects they would hate to lose? Whose pictures do they carry in their wallet or on their phone?

31 Are there any occasions when they lie? If they do, how do they feel about it?

32 What phrases do they commonly use, including curse-words?

33 What's their humour personality?

34 Do they usually feel strong and confident? Or rarely? Who makes them feel in control – and who doesn't?

You also might like to group your character's traits and troubles using the Johari Window. Originally developed as a self-awareness tool, it analyses a character in terms of four facets. Draw a square and divide it into four. In the first, write the things the character and everyone else knows about themselves. In the second, record the 'blind self' – things everyone else knows about the character but he/she doesn't. In the third, explore their hidden self – talents, feelings and secrets that only the character knows. The final window is for the unknown self – abilities, feelings, traits and fears that neither the character nor anyone else suspects. These might emerge in the course of the story.

Fuel the story

Have you identified a frustration, a goal or an ambition? This is crucial. Kurt Vonnegut famously says every character should want something, even if it's only a glass of water. Moreover, this need should present a challenge. Nancy Kress singles out frustration as the supreme force that drives a story. If the character can't get what they want or need, or prevent something, this pushes them out of their comfort zone. It also gives them a reason to continue when their quest gets tough.

Could that frustration come from conflict, where they need to make an impossible choice and will lose either way?

Once you've identified these obstacles, how does your character handle them? The common negative responses to frustration are anger, aggression, giving up, losing confidence, becoming bitter, ill or depressed, numbing the negative emotions with drink, drugs or other self-destructive habits. Equally, they might respond positively, directing the energy into something else or firming their resolve to succeed. This will depend on the character's personality and temperament.

Find out what your characters want and why that will be a challenge.

Imagine you met the character

If you're chatting to a stranger at a wedding, what questions do you ask to get your bearings (aside from how they know the bride and groom)? Some of us would want to know about hobbies, number of children, where they go on holiday, what TV they like, what bands they listen to. What would this character tell you? What is their manner? Do you feel they're lying, exaggerating, fabricating, competing with you or being modest? Do they engage with you or put up a wall? Are they nervous or over-eager to connect?

Watch them talk to someone else. How do they behave now?

The questions we ask strangers reflect our priorities and assumptions, so what does your character want to know when they first meet someone? Is that different from what you'd ask them?

Mystery novelist John E Simpson encountered a variation of this at a workshop taught by science fiction author David Gerrold.

Writers were told to imagine they were in a theatre's wardrobe department and to choose something for a character to wear. They were asked to describe its size, whether it was a period costume, formal, casual, new or threadbare. They added make-up, including expression lines, scars, blemishes and hair. Next was lighting – would they have a strong spotlight, a smoky effect, a highlight of red?

Then the writer had to imagine they were on the stage, facing two chairs. In one would be the character, wearing the gear.

There were more questions. Describe the chairs. Were they both the same? Was one a throne and the other a typing stool? What did the character look like in the flesh? What colour were their eyes? How big were their hands and feet? Was their posture erect, stooped, were they well-groomed or slovenly?

The writer was told to sit in the other chair. The character would look at them. What was their expression? Curious, baleful, resentful, enigmatic?

'Finally,' says Simpson, 'your character leans forward, elbows on knees perhaps. He opens his mouth and says one thing to you. What is their voice like? What does he say?

'I cannot begin to tell you how much that freaked me out. Hair standing up on forearms, all that. When the lights came up, Gerrold just said, "Now write; until you're done." '

Playing favourites

Some of the dullest questions on character design questionnaires are the 'favourites'. Favourite colour, favourite food ... Of course it's handy to have a few trivialities ready to distinguish a character, but favourites don't have to be superficial.

Take, for instance, a character who wears black all the time. Maybe they chose it for its slimming effect, but they could just as easily want simple outfit choices when they rise at 5am. When teenagers go noir, that might be because of a Goth or tragic phase, or it might be because they like the strong statement of a strict personal style, in a colour they haven't worn much until then.

A character may have a favourite food but the preference may be nothing to do with tastebuds. Perhaps it reminds them of a time or a person. Or they might not even have a favourite because no food has ever become that important to them.

Use favourite colours, foods, songs etc to discover a character's depths and highlight parts of their history.

Swap the career stereotypes

Careers may suggest certain personality traits, but if we're not careful we might create stereotypes.

So a soldier is expected to be tough, loyal, physically brave, a team player and self-disciplined. A schoolteacher will be outgoing, stressed, good at speaking in front of audiences, methodical and firm. A writer is sensitive, a nightbird, a loner, nosy about their friends' lives. (You're all fodder for a novel. I thought I'd let you know that.)

Of course, stereotypes arise as a kind of natural selection – because the jobs demand those qualities. But suppose your soldier, teacher or writer didn't have all of them? Doesn't that create interesting possibilities?

This tip comes from romantic suspense author Mary Buckham. She creates lists of her characters' life roles – and then mixes them up. So you decide on five traits for each character, assuming they were the perfect personality profile for that job, and swap the headings around. Isn't it interesting if your schoolteacher is unusually sensitive, a loner and nosy about their friends...

Supporting characters

As we discussed in the earlier section, secondary and peripheral characters don't need so much depth or screen time. But their lives must be independent of the main character.

Crucially, you need to answer these questions –

1 What keeps them busy when the main characters are not around?

2 How do the main characters interfere with them or pull them out of their routine? Perhaps one peripheral character is constantly thwarted or inconvenienced by the main characters, to comic or dramatic effect. Or perhaps a taxi driver or hairdresser finds themselves in a regular confessor role to more major characters.

Other character design games

Various writer friends have shared with me their own quirky solutions when characters are slow to come alive.

The police interview Historical novelist Harriet Smart takes her characters out of the story and puts them in an imaginary police interview. 'I throw a lot of difficult, searching questions at them. You have to answer the questions in the voice or guise of the characters, which can be very revealing. You can work out their motivations and conflicts, and it can be surprising what you come up with. It also avoids the superficiality that questionnaires can produce.'

Free writing Dramatist and novelist James Killick asks himself questions about the characters and scribbles down any answer that comes into his head. 'I do this in my notepad long-hand, which means I'm thinking faster than I'm writing, so end up with a whole heap of ideas. The fact that it's away from the manuscript liberates me, and eventually I'll hit the right answer. Then I return to the text.'

Back story for your eyes only Young adult and middle-grade fiction author Paul Greci writes his characters' back stories up to the point where the novel starts. He's also a keen runner and says he has conversations with his characters while he's clocking up the miles.

For your toolbox

🖋 Questionnaires should prompt you to explore the characters' inner lives, their relationships and how they live.

🖋 Use them as opportunities to change and enrich the plot you have in mind.

🖋 Mine your own internal world to create rounded, unique characters who are not like you.

🖋 Find out how your characters feel about themselves, and the people and places in their present and past.

🖋 Try this: if you met your character, imagine what they would say to you.

🖋 Use favourite colours, foods, songs etc to discover a character's depths and highlight key parts of their history.

🖋 Play with stereotype qualities to find out where your characters fit – and don't fit – into the story world.

🖋 If your characters aren't coming to life, try the police interview, free writing or inventing back story up until the point your novel starts.

Appendix

Top 10 novice mistakes with characters

Before you find your writing legs, it's easy to misjudge how characters are coming across. In a desperate attempt to make a protagonist likable, novice writers often create an insipid paragon. In a bid for the reader's sympathy, they write a miserable, sore-tempered wretch. These discussions will help you balance vulnerability, troubles and likability and get the reader rooting for your people.

Good characters too saintly

No matter what life throws at them, these characters remain cheerful, forgiving and optimistic and never display a single foible or folly. Often, these writers do a fine job with secondary characters, who don't have to fill the hero role. They might be really good at rogues. But they put their protagonist on a stilted regime of angelic behaviour.

Few people are well balanced and wise all the time, no matter how well educated, accommodating, intelligent or mature. Nobody's endlessly tolerant, especially when others are idiotic or nasty − as they often are in novels. And if they are, we feel we haven't seen the whole of them. Also, we don't find them interesting.

Every character will have comfort zones. These are the situations where they're well-balanced, confident and likable. Outside those are the parts of life they don't handle well. Venture a little way and you find the discomfort zone − harmless bad temper and irritation. I promise you these will make a nice character more human. Wade far enough out and discomfort zone becomes warzone. If you want, you can make a real dent in who they are.

When you have a nice protagonist, prod them into their discomfort zone. They will seem far more likable.

Everybody likes them (so the reader must too)

Writers can be scared to let even one character dislike their protagonist. Indeed, they spend many scenes piling on the love. Characters will talk about how much they admire her (or him), that she's worked so hard and deserves so much. There is not one dissenting voice, not even a grouch who's contrary just because.

It's human nature to want to make up our own mind. There will always be naysayers and contrarians. If you don't put this person in the novel, you offer that role to the reader – which may not be what you want.

While we're at it, although you may want to suggest that your central character is an excellent marriage catch or irresistible, beware. Not everyone can find them attractive. And you can't mitigate that by making them shy and unaware of how gorgeous they are.

So give us a break from relentless worship. Perhaps introduce a character who is less than impressed with your marvellous protagonist. Or have some characters tease them to shrink them to human proportions. It will strengthen your case enormously.

Writer leaves scenes out in case they make us dislike the character

Sometimes the writer is worried the reader will disapprove of the protagonist's actions. Perhaps the plot calls for them to ditch an unexciting lover, steal a friend's partner or take an unwanted puppy to the pound. The writer tries to smuggle the action past the reader, reporting it in a summary, then zipping onwards to positive scenes.

But the reader knows it happened. This is similar to the fine-print situation described earlier, where a writer splices a significant event into the book but the reader doesn't absorb it because there was no follow-through. This time, though, a literary sod's law applies. The writer tries to conceal a deed by rushing it, but the reader will notice. Hey, they'll think. She dumped her boyfriend. That sounds important. Why didn't we see it?

In real life, love might be a tad selfish or cruel. But some genres have expectations and might not tolerate a character who leaves a romantic partner (even if he's dull as a moth). If the action will disastrously taint the character, it can't go in the story – however much you conceal it.

Sometimes writers use such events as a stepping stone to a more important part of the plot. So they despatch the boyfriend and hope the reader won't worry about it. But it might be better to rework the plot so you don't have to do this.

Otherwise, must it go? Some stories will be richer if characters do the indecent thing. If your gut tells you they must, go with it. Don't hide it like fine print in a contract – mentioned but not given natural emphasis.

This is conflict. The character may be breaking their own rules, or making a foolish mistake they can't help. They are crossing into the discomfort zone and possibly beyond.

The worst thing to do is duck out of it altogether. If your protagonist does bad things and you don't want the reader to notice, you need to rethink.

My lovely character hates everyone

Unhappy characters can make dynamic, sympathetic protagonists. They need change. But a little angst goes a long way. And it's easy for a writer to draw it out too far.

I critiqued a novel narrated by a bitterly unhappy teenager. She railed against everything. Bridal shops, billboards, hairdressers and beauty parlours were criticised with dripping sarcasm, alternating with promises to nuke them if she ruled the world. In a controlled dose, that would have been fine – but she ranted on in this register for chapter after chapter, with no respite.

But the book worked much better when the author cut most of the complaining and added scenes where the character talked about what mattered to her. This created a more rounded soul who wanted to do more than moan. She had dreams and aims, which she was likely to act on. Now the reader had something to root for; we felt she deserved to fulfil her potential. In the previous version, the writer was so focused on unhappiness that it appeared the entire book might be plotless ranting.

I navigated this problem myself in *My Memories of a Future Life*. I began with a character who was frustrated – a concert pianist, unable to play because of an injury. At the point we meet her, she is incandescently bad-tempered – prickly, intolerant and, within a short time, rather rude to her flatmate's friend. So I had to show this came from a horrifying hole in her life. I wrote a scene where she is contemplating her future In the dead of night. The real reason for her ennui becomes apparent: she is terrified this will be permanent. This was a bonding moment that made the reader her confidante. I also lightened her with humour, to show her potential in happier times.

Although readers are sympathetic to characters who are unhappy and angry, they become drained by them very quickly. Soften them with humour, a thing that they love or something they fear to lose.

My lovely character has to work with idiots

So your protagonist is frustrated in their job. Usually that's a good way to find common ground with a reader. But some novice writers take the rebel behaviour too far. The character is constantly bickering, sniping, slacking off and being superior. Instead of compiling a dull report, they pick up a manual on scriptwriting. They tell their boss how tedious the company is. They act like they really want to join a rock band. The first question is, why aren't they sacked?

I once saw a TV thriller that stuck in my mind because of a main character who was too cool for his job. They were police officers, and instead of watching the suspect's house, the protagonist was reading a sci-fi novel. One of the other officers said: 'can't you act professionally?' The novel-reading character said, in perfect seriousness: 'when I head the team I'll act like a pro'.

Indeed, he later emerged as the hero maverick – a clear case of the writer indulging him because he should have been out on his rump.

As with the sad, angry characters, writers often go feral when handling frustration – possibly because they're enjoying writing with the brakes off. The characters get too confrontational; they behave like jerks. Now, this can be done with enough wit, originality or irony to be charming and bold. More commonly, it's hard to believe and can come across as sneering at people who accept their frustrating jobs.

And usually the writer doesn't have such a combative aim. They just want to show a square peg who desperately needs to find his square hole.

Frustration is a strong emotion, but these writers are looking at the wrong thing. They know about the sense of being imprisoned, but they haven't noticed how it's handled. Usually it has to be kept in check, and so it surfaces in quieter ways.

Frustrated employees need to keep the job – otherwise (drum roll) it wouldn't be a problem. It pays for the house, the kids' schooling, the vacations. The characters will soak up the worst resentments, revealing them to a trusted few. Perhaps they make a collusive comment to an equally frazzled colleague at the water cooler. Even then they may not dare expose their discontent fully – to other people or even to themselves.

A great model is Frank Wheeler in Richard Yates's *Revolutionary Road,* a suburban company man who thinks he's destined for greater things. The characters do their tedious jobs, with carefully measured moments when they let off steam.

Frustrated people often have conflicted feelings about their situation. The character might simultaneously want to hurl their laptop off the roof and be a good company man to get the promotion.

Prose is the perfect medium to explore this gnawing desperation. Movies and TV might have to reduce it to a single scene where the hero pours boiling coffee in the office rubber plant, but in a novel, you can spread it through the bedrock.

There's no truth in frustrated employees acting like hip rebels – unless we are joining them on the day they flip.

Don't make your frustrated characters swagger and rage. Show us what imprisons them and how they tolerate it.

My lovely character is downtrodden but will grow

Many novels are about unassuming characters who are set to blossom. But because of plot or historical constraints, it's not possible to show they have this individual spark.

Indeed she (they are often female) hasn't had the chance to discover it. She has always expected she will become a farmer's wife like her mother. Or go into service like her sisters. She does what she must, apparently content.

Readers will be looking for hints that the status quo will be upset, but where do you put them if the character herself thinks she's satisfied? Often the writer resorts to long scenes of dutiful servitude, as if to ask: 'How would you feel if you were so constrained? Doesn't she deserve to grow?'

She might, but to the reader she looks like she's happy. And happy characters don't look like they will do anything. How do you convince us she has far to go?

These people are like the characters in a frustrating job, but caught at an earlier stop. You need to show that change is likely, even if the character herself doesn't suspect it. When you're boiling a pan of water, a tell-tale rattle warns you something is coming to the surface − so find the bubbles that rise from her unconventional nature. If she's practising the piano, show her improvising instead of sight-reading her strict Victorian tune book. If she's acting *in loco parentis*, show she has desires of her own that she's pushing aside to meet the needs of others.

Fantasies are very important for the character who is making the best of the wrong life. Does she have a secret escape, an activity shared by no one else (or perhaps one special person)? Writing, sitting at an open window when it's raining, borrowing books from the master's library, sketching in front of the paintings in the local art gallery? Something that shows the scope of her soul, that tempts her beyond the bonds she currently submits to.

You need to create a sense of instability, even if the character hasn't recognised it. Show the people, the society and responsibilities that circumscribe her world. And something simmering that won't stay down for ever.

Characters too damaged at start of story

Great characters need an instability, a wound, a need, a missing piece. But presenting that is a tricky balance. Sometimes the writer turns the volume up too far (as we've seen). Sometimes, though, they judge the balance well but start the story too late, when it's hard for the reader to catch up with the protagonist's emotional state.

For instance, the character is a soldier who is having therapy for post-traumatic stress disorder. This is a generalisation, but if we start the story at this point we might have missed several fascinating steps. What if we rewound time a little? Perhaps we could join the character before he seeks help. Maybe he's having reactions he can't explain and is uncomfortable with. He'll try to blank them out and muddle on. Real life will become a battleground. He'll become isolated by his problem.

This isolation is a more powerful way to grip the reader than a character who is already adjusting to his new state.

You might also use this internal battle to add a human dimension in a situation where there isn't room for much character development, as Ian Fleming does with James Bond. Often after Bond has killed he is swamped by feelings of self-loathing. In *Goldfinger* he assassinates a man, then joins a friend for dinner. They're having a convivial time, when Bond feels a wave of violent disgust at the sight of his friend greedily enjoying crab and champagne. Really, though, Bond's submerged self is reminding him that he knows humanity is an animal that eats, kills and dies, regardless of sophisticated living and Dom Perignon.

A person who is in trouble with ordinary life is compelling and memorable — especially in the period before they seek help.

If you show this secret wound, it can engage the reader's empathy and curiosity.

Main character too vulnerable and incapable

Vulnerability is a minefield. Some writers excel at creating protagonists who are deeply troubled. The character is sensitive and sad with a strong internal life, paralysed by strong emotions and insecurity. Perhaps too paralysed, so the writer gives them a responsible occupation. The character works as a bodyguard or brain surgeon or pilot; this proves they have a capable side.

All good, but the writer never shows this capable persona in action. They mention it in an odd line, and focus on the private turmoil.

Here's an example. A character is in such a state of anxiety that she counts the number of strides to the bus stop. She is hopelessly nervous when speaking to a stranger – any stranger. After several chapters, the writer mentions the character is a doctor. And not a doctor disintegrating under pressure, but a doctor who relishes every working day. By then I have it firmly in my head that the character is a hopeless wreck.

I had another writer whose main character seemed similarly prostrated by his troubles. Several chapters in, the writer mentioned the character was also a teacher. And a committed teacher who was popular at his school – not one who was starting to crack.

In both cases, I had to read very closely to discover that the character had a demanding, responsible job. Meanwhile I was worn out because the vulnerability was so relentless and amplified. Furthermore, the information that they were doctors and teachers didn't change my opinion of them. Because I never saw them go to work I assumed they were on sick leave.

The authors didn't intend those effects, of course. Looking in the synopsis I'd find the teacher was supposed to be well-liked and respected. The doctor likewise. But the writers seemed afraid of letting the reader notice this in case it diluted the characters' troubles. Or they thought they should concentrate on the moments that bothered the character most.

Remember we discussed 'show not tell'? Readers retain experiences, not information. If you show us how the character feels desperate, lost, pole-axed by their emotions – that's what we remember. If you mention he's a popular teacher, doctor or firefighter but you don't show it, it's the fine print problem. It gets lost, especially after such vivid emotion. The reader doesn't notice it.

Although secret vulnerability will bond readers to the character, we have to be careful not to make them too needy. Readers often don't notice how much writer does to counter this. Troubled characters are often stronger than you suspect, but it slips past because it's not driving the story. So novice writers either don't put it in, or are afraid to stress it. This usually strips the characters of their dignity and makes them too abject to tolerate. (Readers are cruel.)

If you have made your distressed protagonist strong in other ways, let us know early on. And don't be afraid to make sure the reader notices, with a scene that shows them as capable and respected. It will make them more real and relatable.

Internal conflict is wasted

Some writers tease the reader with a powerful internal conflict but never develop it. The main character has fallen in love but won't commit to a relationship; or they can't choose between two lovers; or they stay in a job that's breaking them; or they want a reconciliation but can't make the first move. The conflict makes the character look interesting and complex – but nothing is done with it.

It's true that some kinds of fiction – especially a series –might present a fundamental inner conflict but never tackle it. It's ongoing background, perhaps insoluble; part of the character's state of life. Indeed, James Bond's slick cocktail of self-loathing is probably what allows him to be such a bastard. It's the tightrope he walks to do the job. If he delves too far he'll come undone and the genre may not tolerate such a big change.

One-off novels, though, tend to beg for these conflicts to be used and explored. But I see many manuscripts where the writer has thrown them in simply to make the major characters interesting. They never develop or cause the characters to do things. That's frustrating for the reader.

These conflicts don't have to reach a state of happy ease. They might burn up in tragedy. On a less drastic level, perhaps they keep churning for ever. But they shouldn't be hidden in the background as a list of 'interesting things that make the character real'. They were part of what attracted readers; we want them to influence what the character does.

If you have kept the conflict low-key or unresolved, was that deliberate? Many writers don't turn the heat up enough. Try asking yourself what would happen if the conflict made life as hard as possible. Take Charlotte Bronte's Jane Eyre – an orphan who possesses nothing but her honesty and integrity. This doesn't cause her much trouble until she seems to get her dearest wish – her employer proposes marriage. All is wonderful until Jane discovers he has another wife. Then, she has a terrible, conflicted decision to make. (Although Bronte relies on convenience for her resolution. She sends Jane away and lets the other characters slug it out. Jane returns to find all objections magically gone and the universe in harmony with her aims. Despite that, I still love the book.) Going back to Jane Eyre's principles, they start as small stubbornnesses that make her interesting and sparky. They get her into moderate trouble. Eventually they force her into a rending decision – she can either live in disgrace and be happy, or stick to her principles. Part of the story's power is this exquisite tension.

Internal conflict could generate your entire story, as in Shakespearean tragedy. Iago and Othello are both proud, ambitious men with interesting, remarkable traits. It all gets uncomradely when Iago is passed over for promotion. Another man might have shrugged it off, but Iago can't. It rocks his sense of who he is and what he deserves. He begins a bid for revenge – all because he feels so bitter.

If you tempt the reader in with a character's conflicted situation, don't leave it as background. Make it generate some of the story.

Character's sudden emotional change has no consequences

Change is good. It shows us that a character's experience mattered. Sometimes, though, a protagonist has a drastic emotional change, then carries on exactly as before. A cop who is normally fearless makes a routine arrest and is paralysed by nerves. In the next scene, he'll go on with his day, without even pausing for thought. The anxiety attack never happens again. Meanwhile the reader is waiting for consequences.

The writer has forgotten there will be fallout after this startling moment. They've aimed only for fireworks and surprise. And it's worked superbly − but they've forgotten to do the rest.

In real life, if a person inexplicably loses their nerve, two things would happen. First, they'd have a reaction, even if they pretended everything was all right. Second, the incident would continue to cause problems. Indeed it would be a significant part of the story. Even if the panic state never returned, they would no longer trust their reactions, especially if it would affect their job or ability to protect their loved ones. If these consequences are missing, it looks very peculiar.

Sometimes but not always – these revelations have been added after the first draft. Perhaps the writer thought of them while revising, or an editor or critique group suggested them. Maybe (as in an earlier discussion) they're trying to add complexity, to demonstrate that the character isn't as straightforward as they seem. But these ideas are too potent to be dismissed so casually. They don't work unless they soak into the whole book. A swift line, paragraph or isolated scene won't be enough, especially with an idea that must have hefty repercussions. Otherwise it's the fine print problem. (Show not tell.)

Romantic or sexual attraction is another type of development that tends to get this drive-through treatment. Again, this is possibly because writers add it as an afterthought. So we'll read a scene where a character has luxuriant fantasies about his best friend's wife. We're surprised, just as the writer intended. But it's never developed. The character continues the book's adventures as though he'd never had such a thought.

When I ask the writer what they were aiming for, they confirm they want Mr A to develop feelings for Mrs B, and for the reader to be aware of it. But the reader won't be if the character isn't. Even if Mr A will never act on his impulse, it must leave an echo. The writer needs to edit that in to explore the idea. Perhaps Mr A is tormented by temptation, or tries to dismiss it as foolish, or decides he'd better buy a red Porsche. What it can't do is vanish.

A startling emotional change isn't enough in itself, even if it surprises the reader. You have to make it feel real, with consequences that trail through the rest of the story.

Can we spot which character is based on real life?

Yes we can. There are two ways that using a real person can go wrong (apart from being sued).

The first is when one character is more nuanced than the others. Or they might be more quirky and distinctive, especially in dialogue, while everyone else conforms to an average. It is as if that character has been designed on a different scale from the rest of the story's people. They might be talked about more frequently than other characters, and maybe admired or loathed more.

Conversely, writers sometimes fail to develop the characters they base on real life. The rest of the cast will be created in three dimensions, with private troubles, a history and dilemmas. Except for one major character, who they seem unwilling to speculate about and is indistinct, or seems to have only external characteristics. Talent, beauty and wit (or their opposites) may make a person stand out in real life, but a novel is an internal medium and your characters must be interesting in their hearts.

Perhaps that's another reason to invent them all from scratch.

Also, central characters need to be carefully tailored. Is your interesting acquaintance really the perfect person to confront the trials of the plot? Can you magnify their flaws or invent new ones? Might you feel more free if you created somebody new?

That's not to say real people can't make great fictional characters. They can also be terrific inspiration if you isolate a few interesting features and invent the rest. But remember to make the other characters just as authentic. It looks uneven if you give a character extra detail, dimension, love and attention.

If you have based a character on someone in real life, don't be afraid to improve on the raw material. And be sure to make the other players equally as vivid.

🖊 When you have a pleasant protagonist, prod their discomfort zone. They will seem far more likable if they're not perfect.

🖊 If everybody likes your good guys, introduce a character who doesn't.

🖊 Even if a character is gorgeous, make sure one character doesn't agree.

🖊 If your protagonist does bad things and you don't want the reader to notice, you need to rethink.

🖊 Although readers are sympathetic to characters who are unhappy and angry, they become drained by them very quickly. Soften them with a little humour or a thing that they love.

🖊 Don't make your frustrated characters swagger and rage. Show us what imprisons them and how they tolerate the status quo.

🖊 Liven up downtrodden characters with a hint of inner spark.

🖊 A secret wound is intriguing for a reader – have you made the most of it?

🖊 Although vulnerability helps us engage with a central

character, don't forget to show us their strengths so they keep their dignity.

- If you tempt the reader in with a character's conflicted situation, don't leave it as background. Make the conflict generate some of the story.

- If you introduce a significant change in a character, it has to reverberate through the entire text from that moment, not be kept as an isolated scene.

- Readers spot if you're favouring a character with extra detail, dimension, love and attention.

- Good central characters are the perfect person to confront the trials of your plot. If you base them on people you know, you might have to adjust their characteristics.

Afterword

All writers are different. We all need ways to get familiar with our characters. For some, that will mean designing them with questionnaires, interviews, recreating their wedding list and the most treasured items from their attic. Others will plunge into the story, getting to know them as they act, perhaps writing exploratory scenes that they wipe later. And of course, a character becomes more vivid once they've rubbed along with others, taken action and made decisions.

A word of caution: sometimes writers shoehorn in everything they have produced when they created a character, even where it may clutter the narrative. Use only what is strictly necessary as the story unfolds. Not a drop more. Don't worry about how much background you're leaving out. It is the 90% of the iceberg that allows you to write with dignity, as Ernest Hemingway would say.

I don't mind leaving the last word to him. Have fun.

About the author

Roz Morris has more than a dozen published novels under her belt. She has a secret identity as a ghostwriter and her titles have sold more than 4 million copies worldwide. She is also coming out of the shadows with critically acclaimed novels of her own: *My Memories of a Future Life* and *Lifeform Three*.

Roz is also a tutor on the *Guardian* newspaper self-publishing courses and mentors other writers. One manuscript she doctored in early form won the Roald Dahl Funny Prize 2012. She began her *Nail Your Novel* series in response to the most common problems her clients encounter.

Another *Nail Your Novel* book is in the works, and Roz always has novels of her own to nail. Connect with her on Twitter at @Roz_Morris and on her blog www.nailyournovel.com

If you've enjoyed this book, would you consider leaving a review on line? It makes all the difference to independent publishers who rely on word of mouth to get their books known. Thank you!

Index

Nail Your Novel: Why Writers Abandon Books and How You Can Draft, Fix and Finish With Confidence

'Should be used as a text in writing courses'
'There are shedloads of books on how to write novels, and a lot are longer and considerably less useful'

Are you writing a novel? Do you want to make sure you finish? Will you get lost and fizzle out? Will you spend more time reading about how to write than getting words down?

Most books on novel-writing make you read hundreds of pages about arcs, inciting incidents, heroes' journeys. It's great to know that – but that's not writing your book.
In 10 steps *Nail Your Novel* will tell you how to:
❖ shape your big idea and make a novel out of it
❖ use research
❖ organise your time
❖ write when you don't feel inspired
❖ reread what you've written and polish it.

You don't even need to read the whole book before you get started. You read a section, then do as it says. And, once you're finally satisfied, *Nail Your Novel* will tell you how to present it to publishers and agents, should you wish to. You've dreamed of writing a novel. Don't procrastinate with another theory book. Don't launch in, get stuck and throw your hard work in a drawer. Draft, fix and finish with confidence.

Available in e-editions and in print.

Writing Plots with Drama, Depth & Heart:
Nail Your Novel 3

'Packed with helpful and targeted advice. The best so far in the Nail Your Novel series.'
'Extremely helpful reference on how to produce a compelling, riveting novel.'

Where do you find story ideas? What's your personal vision? Do you know what genre you are best suited to write? What is literary fiction and how do you write that? How will you give your book depth without seeming preachy or bringing the plot to a standstill? What are the hidden structural patterns that ply the reader's emotions, regardless of your genre or style?

How can you use them with originality?

Where should you play your best twists - and what should they be? How can you write each scene so it holds the reader's curiosity? If you want to write a story that breaks with convention but still keeps readers riveted, how do you do it?

Discover where your best ideas are hiding and how to tell stories with drama, depth and heart.

Available in e-editions and in print.

My Memories of a Future Life

'Genius premise, skilled storytelling

If your life was somebody's past, what echoes would you leave in their soul? Could they be the answers you need now? It's a question Carol never expected to face. She's a gifted musician who needs nothing more than her piano. She certainly doesn't think she's ever lived before. But forced by injury to stop playing, she fears her life may be over. Enter her soulmate Andreq; healer, liar, fraud and loyal friend. Is he her future incarnation or a psychological figment? And can his story help her discover how to live now?

Lifeform Three

'In the great tradition of Atwood and Bradbury'

Misty woods; abandoned towns; secrets in the landscape; a forbidden life by night; the scent of bygone days; a past that lies below the surface; and a door in a dream that seems to hold the answers.

Paftoo is a 'bod', made to serve. He is a groundsman on the last remaining country estate, once known as Harkaway Hall - now a theme park. Paftoo holds scattered memories of the old days but they are regularly deleted to keep him productive. When he starts to have dreams of the old days and his cherished connection with Lifeform Three, Paftoo is propelled into a nocturnal battle to reclaim his memories, his former companions and his soul.

Available in ebook, paperback and audiobook

CPSIA information can be obtained at www.ICGtesting.com
Printed in the USA
BVOW03s1313080415

395305BV00001B/4/P